Mem'ries Sweet, Comrades True

Mem'ries Sweet, Comrades True

Favorite Recipes from Members of the TCU Retirees Association

TCURA

TCU Press
Fort Worth, Texas

LCCN

2021048160

TCU Press

Fort Worth, Texas

TCU Box 298300

Fort Worth, Texas 76129

To order books: 1.800.826.8911

Design by Bill Brammer

This book is dedicated to TCU retirees. This group, including both retired faculty and staff, has helped build TCU into the quality institution that receives worldwide recognition today.

Contents

Acknowledgments

A number of people helped make this cookbook a reality. The cookbook committee would like to acknowledge them here for their help and advice.

First, the cookbook was Larry Adams's brainchild, so we thank him for launching this effort and supporting us. We also appreciate the TCU-RA board for their encouragement and support of this project.

Dr. Anne VanBeber of Nutrition who, with the help of her administrative assistant, Meggan Duncan, and two of her students, Charlie Tapkin and Dalia Richmond, did the work of getting nutrition labels for each recipe. Dr. VanBeber also contributed the healthy substitutions appendix.

Robert Carter of TCU's Marketing and Communication department helped us find pictures of the campus that were used throughout this book.

Laura Meyn, a cookbook author, consulted with us throughout the development of the book. Her help was invaluable.

We thank TCU Press for supporting this book.

And, finally, Judy Groulx saved the day by converting nutrition labels into a readable format.

THE TCURA COOKBOOK COMMITTEE

Dr. Julie Baker, *Committee Chair*

Susan Adams

Jean Andrus

Dr. Sharon Fairchild

Dr. Stan Hagadone

Dr. Jane Mackay

Nancy Madsen

Judy Oelfke Smith

Introduction

Society's focus on food and cooking has been increasing over the years. This interest is evident in the sheer number of TV cooking shows, the number of print cookbooks displayed in bookstores, and the many online resources. It reflects the growing personal satisfaction men and women find in preparing home-cooked food. It is hoped that this book of favorite recipes from members of the TCU Retirees Association (TCURA) will be of interest to all of those individuals who find joy in cooking.

Many of the recipes are favorites that have been passed from generation to generation. Other recipes may show more current trends, such as an emphasis on nutrition and healthy eating. The book is enriched with accompanying personal memories about each dish. As in TCU's Alma Mater Hymn, these "mem'ries sweet" accompany recipes from TCU faculty, staff, family, and friends—"comrades true."

The cookbook is a collaborative effort. Each recipe includes a nutritional analysis by Dr. Anne VanBeber and her students in the Department of Nutrition Science. Dr. VanBeber has also provided an appendix containing suggested recipe substitutions for healthy deliciousness. TCU's Marketing & Communication department chose photos of the campus, including historic buildings and scenes, used throughout the book, and TCU Press produced the volume you hold in your hands.

The members of the TCURA Cookbook Committee hope that each recipe and accompanying story will be an invitation to experience food that has warmed generations of Horned Frogs and their families.

The TCURA Mission Statement

The Texas Christian University Retirees Association exists to provide opportunities for fellowship, to promote lifelong learning, to advocate for fair benefits, to recognize the accomplishments of its members, and to strengthen the relationship between the retirees and the university.

A History of the TCU Retirees Association 1983–present

John Perkins, president of the TCURA in 1989–1990, wrote an initial history of the organization. He wrote, "When Jeff Horn retired from the School of Education in 1981, it seemed to him that a veritable gulf opened between retirees and the university. This was true even though there were some university privileges available, but no organization either for social or other benefits. Jeff was encouraged primarily by Troy Crenshaw and Comer Clay to undertake the study of a possible organization." Jeff became the first president in 1983.

From the beginning there were monthly luncheons and newsletters during the school year as well as a Christmas luncheon. Executive Council meetings were held in the homes of members until recently. The initial Christmas luncheons were held in Weatherly Hall in the basement of Brite Divinity School.

Monthly luncheons were originally held at Colonial Jetton's Cafeteria on Rogers Road across from where the Woodshed is now.

In our Mission Statement, approved in 2014, the TCU Retirees Association exists to promote opportunities for fellowship, lifelong learning, advocacy for fair benefits, recognition of members, and the relationship between the retirees and the university.

From its founding, TCURA has been an advocate for retiree benefits, especially health benefits. This was never more pertinent than in 2013–14, when the university tried to reduce prescription drug benefits, and the Retirees Association and others on campus fought to have the current "bridge" program instated through 2019. In 2019 another committee was formed to study what benefits may look like beyond the end of the bridge program.

Accomplishments of the organization in past years include the following:

2014 – When Jean Walbridge was president, she chaired an ad hoc committee with Stan Hagadone and Mary Lane to create our Mission Statement.

• We joined the Association of Retirement Organizations in Higher Education (AROHE) and sent Jean Walbridge to its biannual meeting.

2015 – Through the chancellor's support, TCURA became a budgeted unit of the university and moved both Executive Council meetings and monthly luncheons to the Kelly Center.

• Larry Adams chaired a committee to update our constitution and bylaws, which were approved and are available on our website.

• We created a master roster with over six hundred individuals on it from the various email and snail mail lists that were available. Thanks to Judy Groulx for serving as our List Master.

2016 – In an effort to increase brand awareness, we had a logo created, developed a brochure that is sent to new retirees and available at HR, and we created our own website—tcura.tcu.edu.

• We initiated a voluntary donor program to support TCURA's ever-expanding programs and activities.

• Stan Hagadone and Larry Adams represented us at AROHE, and Janet George Herald and Julie Baker attended in 2018.

2018 – "A TCU Treasure" award was created and awarded for the first time in 2018. Initial awardees were Emmet Smith and Manny Reinecke; 2019 recipients were Chuck Lamb and Ron Flowers.

The TCURA has been a vibrant and ever-growing organization that we should be very proud of. It's clear across the years that the collegial environment of TCU not only created but has helped support this organization. And we look forward to a bright future.

(Special thanks to Janet George Herald for her extensive research on TCURA history, which is included in this article.)

Rose Bowl Celebration. Texas Christian University.
Photo by Glen E. Ellman.

TCU Rose Bowl Helmet in Parade. Texas Christian University.
Photo by Glen E. Ellman.

APPETIZERS AND BEVERAGES

Bloody Mary Mix

"At History Department parties during our thirty years at TCU, we often served Bloody Marys from a recipe we brought from Chapel Hill, NC. However, times have changed, so the recipe now has been reduced to just four servings. It is still the best Bloody Mary mix I've ever tasted, and you can double the quantities if you want to serve more people."

Sally Landis Bohon, Honors Program

Makes 4 servings

¼ cup chopped onion
¼ cup chopped green pepper
¼ cup chopped celery
1 Tbsp. sugar
1 tsp. salt
1 bay leaf, crumbled
1 Tbsp. Worcestershire sauce
½ tsp. horseradish (more or less to taste)
2 to 4 dashes Tabasco
2 Tbsp. cider vinegar
2 cups tomato juice *(Dei Fratelli in a carton, if you can find it, because it's not made from concentrate, but any tomato juice will do.)*

Chop the vegetables into ¼-inch dice and put them into a quart Mason jar. Add the rest of the ingredients except the tomato juice to the vegetables and stir together. Then pour in the tomato juice. Stir to mix. Cover with lid or plastic wrap and refrigerate for 24 hours. Strain into serving pitcher. You can use the vegetables over for a second batch.

Fortunately, this keeps for a couple of days in the refrigerator because it is unlikely you will be drinking it all at once. But it is great as a "Virgin Mary," which is straight, without any alcohol. For a Bloody Mary, fill a highball glass half up with ice, add a jigger or two of vodka, and fill with

Recipe Continues

the strained juice. Stir to mix. It will not be nearly so festive, though, if you do not add a garnish—celery sprig, pickled okra, or olives on a stick. You can cap it off with a cooked peeled shrimp. In fact, with a big enough glass you can pack a light lunch on a stick with one of each of the above. Makes one pint.

PER SERVING: Calories 37; Fat 0.1 g (Saturated 0 g); Cholesterol 0 mg; Sodium 914 mg; Carbohydrate 9.3 g; Fiber 0.8 g; Sugars 7.9 g; Protein 1.1 g

Ceviche

"We love this version of ceviche and think it is the addition of green olives that sets it apart. It is also very simple to make."

Donna Johnson, Executive Assistant to the Provost

Makes 6 servings

1 lb. tilapia, cut into small chunks
25 to 30 limes
1 small jar green stuffed olives, chopped
½ cup olive oil
2 to 3 fresh tomatoes, diced
½ onion, diced
1 jalapeno, diced small
1 tsp. chopped cilantro
salt and pepper to taste

Place tilapia chunks into bowl and squeeze limes until juice covers fish. Mix and place in freezer for about an hour. Lime juice will cook the fish. When fish is opaque, add other ingredients, stir well, chill, and serve.

PER SERVING: Calories 405; Fat 0.1 g (Saturated 28.8 g); Cholesterol 37 mg; Sodium 141 mg; Carbohydrate 31.9 g; Fiber 8.5 g; Sugars 6.2 g; Protein 16.5 g

Cherry Dip

"The northwest corner of Michigan's lower peninsula has beautiful clear lakes, maple and pine forests, and sand dunes all along the shore of Lake Michigan. It's a perfect environment for growing cherries, but we're not just making jams and pies with them. Dried cherries are like big plump raisins, wonderful in salads and sauces. This dip is delicious with crackers or with a plate of crunchy raw vegetables."

Judy Groulx, Emeritus Associate Professor, College of Education

Serves 8

1 cup dried tart cherries, chopped small
½ cup crumbled blue cheese
½ cup chopped walnuts
1 cup sour cream
¼ cup mayonnaise

Combine all ingredients. Serve on crackers or veggies.

PER SERVING: Calories 505; Fat 48 g (Saturated 18 g); Cholesterol 80 mg; Sodium 667 mg; Carbohydrate 38.2 g; Fiber 8.5 g; Sugars 5 g; Protein 11 g

Colin's Queso

"I got this recipe from a TCU employee whose name escapes me now, but she was a source of a lot of good recipes, particularly for appetizers. I used to put corn chips in a bowl and ladle this over it for supper when my kids were teens. The oldest, Colin, particularly loved it, hence the name."

Judy Alter, Director, TCU Press

Recipe Continues

Serves 4 to 6

1 lb. hamburger meat
1 lb. sausage (mild or hot, your choice)
1 lb. Velveeta cheese
1 (10.5-oz.) can cream of mushroom soup
1 (8-oz.) jar Pace picante sauce (mild or hot, your choice)

Brown hamburger meat and sausage, breaking up chunks until crumbly. Drain and put in a slow cooker. Cut Velveeta in chunks and add to the cooker. Add mushroom soup and picante sauce.

PER SERVING: Calories 653; Fat 45.4 g (Saturated 19.3 g); Cholesterol 175 mg; Sodium 2240 mg; Carbohydrate 13.3 g; Fiber 1 g; Sugars 8.1 g; Protein 48.9 g

Corn Dip

"This recipe for corn dip is Pat Miller's favorite! It was served at most every party in the Registrar's Office."

Melinda Rubenkoenig, Classroom Scheduler, Registrar's Office

Serves 6

2 (11-oz.) cans Mexican corn, drained
2 (4.5-oz.) cans chopped green chilies
½ cup mayonnaise
½ cup sour cream
2 cups grated cheese
5 dashes tabasco
1 tsp. garlic powder

Recipe Continues

1 tsp. cayenne pepper
1 package Frito's corn chips (scoops)

Mix all ingredients except corn chips in a medium bowl. Serve with chips.

PER SERVING: Calories 474; Fat 27.4 g (Saturated 11.9 g); Cholesterol 53 mg; Sodium 565 mg; Carbohydrate 46.9 g; Fiber 12.8 g; Sugars 20 g; Protein 16 g

Easy Chicken Liver Pâté

"This recipe is somewhat forgiving. Enjoy!"

Joe Bobich, Emeritus Professor, Chemistry

Serves 4

8 Tbsp. (1 stick) unsalted butter, cubed
2 medium shallots, peeled and chopped
1 pint or 1 lb. (approximately) chicken livers, trimmed and any green (bile) removed
1 Tbsp. fresh chopped thyme, or 1 tsp. dried
⅓ cup port or Madeira
1 tsp. heavy cream
Kosher salt to taste

Melt 4 Tbsp. butter in a frying pan over medium heat. Add shallots and sauté until translucent. Be careful not to burn. Add livers, thyme, and Madeira or port and turn heat to high. Stir pan contents until the livers are brown on the outside, but pink and soft on the inside (about 5 minutes). Be careful not to overcook. Turn off heat and transfer pan contents to a food processor or blender. Add cream and the remain-

Recipe Continues

ing butter. Puree until smooth. Taste and adjust seasoning. Pour into a deep dish and smooth the top with a spatula. Cover and chill until firm. Freeze or consume within 4 or 5 days. Serve with toast or crackers.

PER SERVING: Calories 453; Fat 34.6 g (Saturated 19.5 g); Cholesterol 715 mg; Sodium 256 mg; Carbohydrate 5.2 g; Fiber 0 g; Sugars 0 g; Protein 28.7 g

Eggnog

"Served in a pretty punch bowl, this recipe, given to us by a friend while we were stationed in Japan in the Air Force, has cheered us many a Christmas Eve."

Mary Lane, Assistant to the Dean, School of Education

Serves 6

6 eggs
¾ cup sugar
1 pint heavy cream
1 pint milk
1 cup rum (dark) or brandy

Separate egg whites from yolks. Beat ½ cup granulated sugar into the yolks. Whip the cream and stir it and the milk into the egg mixture. Slowly stir in the rum (taste before adding all). Set aside for 3 to 4 hours to ripen. When ready to serve, beat the egg whites with ¼ cup sugar and fold into yolk mixture. Sprinkle with nutmeg.

PER SERVING: Calories 559; Fat 35.6 g (Saturated 20.8 g); Cholesterol 280 mg; Sodium 131 mg; Carbohydrate 31.6 g; Fiber 0 g; Sugars 29.1 g; Protein 9.9 g

Horned Frog Popcorn

"This is a fun snack for tailgating. It's easy to make and festive. I obtained the recipe while in a waiting room at M.D. Anderson Hospital in Houston. A lady near me had a bag of red and white corn. She told me how to make it. Any flavor of Jell-O may be used, but purple is best when the Horned Frogs are playing!"

Mary Jo Clegg, spouse of Luther Clegg, Emeritus Professor of Education

Serves 4

8 cups popped corn (remove any un-popped kernels)
salt
⅓ cup butter
1 (3-oz.) package grape Jell-O

Lightly salt popped corn. Melt butter and pour over popped corn, mixing thoroughly to spread butter on all the corn. Sprinkle with Jell-O and mix again to spread color on corn.

PER SERVING: Calories 435; Fat 32.1 g (Saturated 19.6 g); Cholesterol 81 mg; Sodium 260 mg; Carbohydrate 34.5 g; Fiber 4.6 g; Sugars 9.8 g; Protein 5.5 g

Hot Roast Beef Party Sandwiches

"I served these hot roast beef sandwiches at a party. My son, Ryan, and his wife, Tiffany, served them during a gathering of their TCU Class of 2003 alumni friends. The sandwiches were a huge hit, and the recipe was shared with all who enjoyed them!

Melinda Rubenkoenig, Classroom Scheduler, Registrar's Office

Recipe Continues

Serves 12 to 16

½ cup finely chopped walnuts or pecans
2 (9.25-oz.) packages dinner rolls (I use the Hawaiian dinner rolls)
⅔ cup peach preserves
½ cup mustard/mayonnaise blend (Hellmann's Dijonnaise mustard)
¾ lb. thinly sliced deli roast beef, chopped (deli sliced ham, turkey, or chicken is also good)
½ lb. thinly sliced Havarti cheese
salt and pepper to taste (optional)

Bake at 325°. Heat nuts in a small nonstick skillet over medium-low heat, stirring occasionally, 5 to 6 minutes or until lightly roasted. (When you start to smell the aroma of the nuts, they are roasted. They will burn really fast.) Remove rolls from packages. Do not separate rolls. Cut rolls in half horizontally, creating 1 top and 1 bottom layer per package. Spread preserves on cut sides of top layer of rolls, sprinkle with nuts. Spread mustard-mayonnaise blend on cut sides of bottom layer of rolls, top with beef and cheese. Sprinkle with salt and pepper to taste, if desired. Cover with top halves of rolls, preserves sides down, and wrap in aluminum foil. Bake for 20 to 25 minutes or until cheese is melted. Slice into individual sandwiches.

Note: To make ahead, prepare recipe as directed but do not bake. Freeze up to 1 month. Thaw overnight in refrigerator and bake as directed.

PER SERVING: Calories 243; Fat 0.1 g (Saturated 4.1 g); Cholesterol 35 mg; Sodium 254 mg; Carbohydrate 24.7 g; Fiber 8.6 g; Sugars 8.6 g; Protein 14 g

Jalapeño Squares

"I don't know where I got this recipe, but I have taken it to many parties through the years, and it has really been a great appetizer and hit!"

Sharon Campbell, Administrative Assistant, AddRan College of Liberal Arts

Serves 8 to 12

1 lb. Monterey Jack cheese with jalapeños, grated
1 lb. sharp cheddar cheese, grated
2 eggs, beaten
½ cup all-purpose flour
1 (12-oz.) can evaporated milk

Bake at 350°. In a large bowl, combine the grated cheeses, then press into the bottom of a 9 x 13-in. baking dish. Combine the eggs, flour, and evaporated milk. Pour egg mixture over cheeses. Bake for 30 minutes. Cool slightly and cut into squares. For a spicier version, add chopped jalapeños to the egg mixture.

PER SERVING: Calories 541; Fat 0.1 g (Saturated 25.1 g); Cholesterol 163 mg; Sodium 717 mg; Carbohydrate 11.4 g; Fiber 0.2 g; Sugars 4.9 g; Protein 33.1 g

Homemade Kahlua (decaffeinated)

"Kahlua has been my favorite alcoholic beverage for many years, but I try to stay away from caffeine. When I found this recipe, it solved my dilemma. It also makes a nice gift when poured into attractive bottles. I have given it to many of my TCU friends and hate for them to see how simple it is to make."

Donna Johnson, Executive Assistant to the Provost

Recipe Continues

Serves 6 to 8

1 quart water
3 cups sugar
10 tsp. instant coffee (I use Yuban decaf)
3 cups 100 proof vodka
3 tsp. vanilla

Mix water, sugar, and coffee, then simmer for at least 1 hour (until syrupy). Cool for a couple of hours at room temperature, then add vodka and vanilla. Pour into bottles. No need to refrigerate. Makes approximately 1¾ quarts or 7 cups.

PER SERVING: Calories 532; Fat 0 g (Saturated 0 g); Cholesterol 0 mg; Sodium 5 mg; Carbohydrate 75.2 g; Fiber 0 g; Sugars 75.2 g; Protein 0 g

Mediterranean Layered Dip

"I was having company and needed an appetizer. My favorite foods are Mediterranean, and I had all the ingredients in my refrigerator, so I just layered them on a plate and served with pita chips. It is very easy because all the ingredients are prepared."

JULIE BAKER, Emeritus Professor of Marketing

Serves 6 to 8

1 cup of prepared hummus, any flavor
1 to 2 Tbsp. prepared pesto, or to taste
1 to 2 Tbsp. chopped black olives, or tapenade, or to taste
1 to 2 Tbsp. chopped tomatoes, or to taste
1 to 2 Tbsp. feta cheese, crumbled
salt and pepper to taste

Recipe Continues

good extra virgin olive oil to taste
pita chips

Layer all ingredients except pita chips in the order listed on a shallow dish or plate. Serve with pita chips.

PER SERVING: Calories 130; Fat 8.4 g (Saturated 1.6 g); Cholesterol 3 mg; Sodium 305 mg; Carbohydrate 9.5 g; Fiber 3.9 g; Sugars 0.4 g; Protein 5.7 g

Stuffed Jalapeños

"These are a favorite at our TCU tailgate! They can be prepared the night before, refrigerated, and popped in the oven before heading to the stadium to cheer on the Frogs. Only 4 ingredients, low carb, and delicious!"

JANET GEORGE HERALD, Associate Dean of Admissions

Serves 8 to 12

1 lb. ground sausage
1 (8-oz.) package cream cheese, softened
1 cup grated Parmesan cheese
28 to 30 jalapeños

Bake at 425°. Cook sausage in skillet until browned. Set aside. Mix cream cheese with Parmesan cheese. Add cooked sausage and mix well. Rinse jalapeños. Cut each jalapeño in half lengthwise and remove seeds. Be careful not to get juice in your eyes. Stuff jalapeños with sausage mixture. Bake on a large cookie sheet for 20 minutes until tops are golden brown.

PER SERVING: Calories 396; Fat 32.3 g (Saturated 15.4 g); Cholesterol 99 mg; Sodium 769 mg; Carbohydrate 4.6 g; Fiber 1.4 g; Sugars 1.8 g; Protein 22.8 g

Founders of TCU: Addison and Randolph Clark. TCU Marketing and Communication. *Photo by Carolyn Cruz.*

BREAKFAST AND BREADS

Abbey Rose Bed and Breakfast Scones

"The Abbey Rose B&B was located in beautiful Victoria, Canada. The scones are especially popular on field trips with our birding friends."

MARY LANE, Assistant to the Dean, School of Education

Serves 8

2 cups all-purpose flour or 2 cups whole-wheat flour
⅓ cup sugar (less sugar for whole-wheat cheese scones—approximately ¼ cup)
1 tsp. baking powder
½ tsp. baking soda
⅓ cup cold butter
⅓ cup frozen or dried fruit (blueberries, currants, apricots) or cheese if making whole-wheat scones
⅔ cup buttermilk

Bake at 350°. Sift or mix all dry ingredients together. Cut ⅓ cup cold butter into flour mixture. Add fruit (or cheese) and buttermilk into flour mixture. Stir until mixture clings together. Form tablespoon-size clumps on a cookie sheet. Bake for approximately 20 minutes.

PER SERVING: Calories 243; Fat 8.2 g (Saturated 5 g); Cholesterol 21 mg; Sodium 156 mg; Carbohydrate 39.1 g; Fiber 1.2 g; Sugars 14 g; Protein 4 g

My Favorite Banana Bread

"A longtime family friend gave me this recipe. Each time I serve it, I get requests for a copy of the recipe. It is easy, and the ingredients are usually on hand. I keep several loaves in the freezer."

JEAN ANDRUS, Administrative Assistant, Harris College of Nursing

Recipe Continues

Serves 12

½ cup (1 stick) softened butter
1¼ cups sugar
2 eggs
3 ripe, mashed bananas
1½ cups flour
4 Tbsp. buttermilk with 1 tsp. baking soda dissolved in it
1 tsp. vanilla
Optional: ½ cup pecans

Bake at 350°. Cream together the butter and the sugar. Add the eggs, bananas, flour, buttermilk mixture, vanilla, and nuts, if using. Bake in greased and floured loaf pan for 1 hour.

PER SERVING: Calories 243; Fat 8.7 g (Saturated 5.2 g); Cholesterol 39.9 mg; Sodium 175 mg; Carbohydrate 39.9 g; Fiber 1.2 g; Sugars 24.8 g; Protein 3.1 g

Breakfast Casserole

"My sister-in-law gave me this recipe many years ago. It is easy and delicious. It has become a holiday breakfast/brunch tradition in our family ever since."

JULIE BAKER, Emeritus Professor of Marketing

Serves 12

1 lb. bulk sausage
1 cup Bisquick, or other baking mix
2 cups milk
4 large eggs
2 cups shredded cheese
salt and pepper to taste

Recipe Continues

Bake at 350°. Brown sausage in frying pan until no longer pink. Layer sausage first, then cheese in a 9 x 13-in. pan. Mix together the rest of the ingredients and pour over sausage mixture. Bake 30 to 45 minutes until done.

You can substitute sautéed vegetables and/or ham for the sausage.

PER SERVING: Calories 289; Fat 20.9 g (Saturated 8.8 g); Cholesterol 117 mg; Sodium 564 mg; Carbohydrate 8.4 g; Fiber 0.2 g; Sugars 3.2 g; Protein 16.2 g

Cottage Cheese Pancakes

"This recipe is from a neighbor in Minnesota. Almost every day when we arrived home, she would call from her kitchen window, 'coffee's on.' Of course, that usually turned out to be supper. Before we moved, she let me go through her recipe box. This is one of my favorites."

Gail Davis, Emeritus Professor of Nursing

Serves 4 to 6

4 eggs, separated
6 heaping Tbsp. flour
1 Tbsp. sugar
½ tsp. salt
¼ cup milk
6 heaping Tbsp. cottage cheese

Beat the egg whites until stiff. Beat egg yolks slightly, add the rest of the ingredients, and mix well. Fold in the beaten egg whites. Cook pancakes on a buttered griddle or pan.

PER SERVING: Calories 147; Fat 5.3 g (Saturated 1.8 g); Cholesterol 167 mg; Sodium 446 mg; Carbohydrate 14.2 g; Fiber 0.3 g; Sugars 4.1 g; Protein 10.5 g

Cottage Cheese Oatmeal Zucchini Pancakes

Karen Stone, Director, Brown-Lupton Gallery and spouse of Howard Stone, Professor of Pastoral Theology, Brite School of Divinity

Serves 4

1 cup cottage cheese
½ cup old-fashioned oatmeal
3 eggs
1 tsp. vanilla
1 to 3 tsp. honey
Approximately 1 cup grated zucchini (1 smallish-medium one) washed, not peeled
Cinnamon to taste
2 Tbsp. whole-wheat flour
Optional: ½ cup cooked oat berries (groats), drained

Preheat griddle to 375° and spray with PAM if griddle isn't nonstick. Mix everything, except the oat groats, in a blender. Pulse until ingredients are mixed, then run on high to make it smooth. If desired, stir in the oat groats, which will add a little "resistance to bite" and make the pancakes slightly heartier. Mixture will be fairly thin. Spoon about 1 Tbsp. of batter on hot griddle for each pancake. Turn when bubbles pop and edges are dry. Remove fairly quickly—as soon as they appear to be done through. (The zucchini will keep them moist even if you overcook some of them.) When the last batch is turned, the cook can unplug the griddle and start eating! Top with sweetened berries or real maple syrup (butter or Parkay spray is optional).

I see no reason why you couldn't substitute other fruits or vegetables (such as acorn squash or apples) for the zucchini, as long as they can be grated and will cook quickly. Just adjust the honey and spice accordingly. These are super healthy pancakes that also taste great, a little cheesecake-y. Make them small, or you will have a big mess.

Recipe Continues

PER SERVING: Calories 144; Fat 4.8 g (Saturated 1.8 g); Cholesterol 127 mg; Sodium 279 mg; Carbohydrate 0.3 g; Fiber 0.9 g; Sugars 2.5 g; Protein 13.3 g

Crescent Rolls

"This recipe for yeast rolls is my family's favorite recipe. I've been making it for nearly fifty years, and it's always on the menu for special dinners. The recipe came from my mother who was an amazing cook. It was a rare meal when she didn't bake homemade bread—biscuits for breakfast, cornbread for supper (dinner), and yeast rolls on Sunday. This dough can also be divided into small balls (about 60) and baked two balls to a cup in greased muffin tins. It can be used as well to make cinnamon and orange rolls."

Mary Jo Clegg, spouse of Luther Clegg, Emeritus Professor of Education

Makes 32 rolls

2 packages dry yeast
⅓ cup warm water (115 to 120°)
½ cup sugar, plus 1 tsp.
1 cup milk
1 tsp. salt
½ cup (1 stick) butter cut into 6 slices, plus extra for rolling and greasing
2 eggs, beaten
5 to 6 cups flour

Bake at 375°. Dissolve yeast in ⅓ cup warm water. Add 1 tsp. sugar and set aside to rest. After about 10 minutes, yeast should be "working" and beginning to form small bubbles. Scald milk and add butter slices, sugar, and salt. Stir to melt butter. When milk mixture has cooled to lukewarm (below 115°), add to yeast. Add beaten eggs and mix well. Add enough flour to make a pliable dough. May take more or less flour. Place dough on floured surface and knead 8 minutes, using more flour as needed to keep dough from sticking. Place dough in greased bowl, turning to

Recipe Continues

grease all sides. Cover and let rise until doubled. Divide dough into four equal portions. Roll each portion into a circle and spread lightly with butter. Cut into 8 long triangles with pizza cutter or sharp knife. Roll into crescents, starting at wide end, rolling toward tip. Place on greased cookie sheets, seam down. Brush tops lightly with melted butter. Cover and let rise. Bake for 12 to 15 minutes, or until tops are golden brown.

PER SERVING: Calories 117; Fat 3.5 g (Saturated 2 g); Cholesterol 18 mg; Sodium 102 mg; Carbohydrate 18.6 g; Fiber 0.6 g; Sugars 3.5 g; Protein 2.8 g

Crustless Quiche

"These quiches are to die for, and probably will kill you, but it's worth it for a family meal. This is one of those recipes that makes you feel really good because there is no crust to make you feel guilty. When you read the ingredients, you realize they have made up for the calorie savings. This recipe makes two quiches, which is great for family breakfasts at Christmas or any other time."

Linda Moore, Emeritus Professor of Social Work

Serves 8 to 10

½ cup (1 stick) butter
½ cup flour
1½ cups milk
2½ cups cottage cheese
1 (12-oz.) pkg. cream cheese
1 tsp. baking powder
1 tsp. salt
1 tsp. Dijon mustard
9 eggs
3 cups shredded Swiss cheese
⅓ cup Parmesan cheese

Recipe Continues

Bake at 350°. Make the white sauce: Melt butter over low heat. Add flour and stir. Gradually add milk and stir until thick. Cool 15 minutes. Mix together the cottage cheese, the cream cheese, baking powder, salt, and mustard. In a separate bowl, beat the eggs. Add cottage cheese mixture and the white sauce, beating constantly. Fold in the shredded Swiss cheese and the Parmesan cheese until smooth. Chill until ready to bake. Pour into two 9-inch pie pans. Bake for 40 minutes. You can freeze these, too.

PER SERVING: Calories 283; Fat 21.3 g (Saturated 12.8 g); Cholesterol 141 mg; Sodium 48.4 mg; Carbohydrate 6.8 g; Fiber 0.1 g; Sugars 1.5 g; Protein 16.5 g

Easy Pecan Rolls

"These rolls were a Christmas gift to our family for many years from my friend, Bobbi Pedersen. When her husband was transferred to Chicago, she shared her recipe, so that our Christmas morning tradition could continue. My children now make these rolls for their families to enjoy on Christmas morning!"

Wendy Crowley, Director, Student Financial Services

Makes 24 rolls

24 frozen (rise and bake) Parker house rolls
1 package vanilla pudding mix (cook and serve style)
1 cup chopped pecans
¾ cup butter
¾ cup brown sugar
sprinkling of cinnamon
¾ cup raisins (optional)

Recipe Continues

Bake at 350°. Place frozen rolls in two greased 8-inch cake pans. Sprinkle rolls with cinnamon and nuts (add raisins here, if desired). Combine melted butter, brown sugar, and pudding mix (equals 1⅓ cups). Pour half of mixture over the top of each pan of frozen rolls (⅔ cup for each pan). Cover pans tightly with foil or plastic lid, and let set on counter at room temperature overnight. By morning rolls will have thawed and risen. Bake for 30 minutes. Remove from oven and invert onto a pan. Serve immediately.

PER SERVING: Calories 563; Fat 35.2 g (Saturated 10.1 g); Cholesterol 33 mg; Sodium 504 mg; Carbohydrate 56.9 g; Fiber 4.5 g; Sugars 25.9 g; Protein 9.5 g

Flashpannkaka

"Shortly after my husband Gayle and I married fifty-four years ago, we spent the night with my mother-in-law, Irene Gilmore. She served this wonderful breakfast dish, and I have been making it on a regular basis all these years! My family really enjoys it. It is also good warmed as a leftover the next morning."

Sharon Campbell, Administrative Assistant, AddRan College of Liberal Arts

Serves 12

½ lb. bacon
5 eggs
3 cups milk
1½ cups all-purpose flour
1 Tbsp. granulated sugar
1 tsp. salt
Melted butter and warm maple syrup (for serving)

Recipe Continues

Bake at 500°. Fry and crumble bacon. Pour grease and crumbled bacon into a 9 x 13-in. metal baking pan. (Do not use glass pan.) Cool. In a large bowl, mix the eggs, milk, flour, sugar, and salt. Pour batter over cooled crumbled bacon and grease in pan. Bake 25 minutes exactly. It will rise, and when removed from oven, it will fall. Cut into squares and serve with melted butter and warm maple syrup. (If you want to cut the recipe in half, it fits in a metal pie pan. Do not use glass pie pan.)

PER SERVING: Calories 220; Fat 11.1 g (Saturated 3.9 g); Cholesterol 94 mg; Sodium 685 mg; Carbohydrate 16.3 g; Fiber 0.4 g; Sugars 3.9 g; Protein 12.9 g

Gluten-free Breakfast Casserole

"This became my favorite go-to brunch recipe when I realized a (wheat) gluten intolerance. Formerly, I used a similar recipe which called for bread cubes rather than hash brown potatoes. Using hash browns from the frozen foods grocery aisle, this recipe featuring a root vegetable additionally saved time and effort."

Laura Adcock, Applications Analyst, Information Technology

Serves 10 to 12

½ lb. meat (e.g. bacon, sausage, ham) or meat substitute
12 eggs
½ cup milk (I use almond milk*)
½ cup water
1 tsp. salt
½ tsp. pepper
¼ tsp. dill weed
1 package (about 16 oz.) hash brown potatoes
(if using frozen potatoes, thaw)
4 oz. sharp cheddar cheese, shredded

Recipe Continues

½ cup onion, chopped (I use green onion, green part only*)
½ cup red (or green) bell pepper, medium, diced

Bake at 375°. Pre-cook meat, if needed, and cut into bite-size pieces. In a large bowl, whisk together the eggs, milk, water, salt, pepper, and dill weed. Add the meat, hash browns, cheese, onion, and bell pepper to the egg mix, combining thoroughly. Pour into a 9 x 13-in. baking dish, spreading the mixture evenly. Bake approximately 30 to 40 minutes, or until a knife inserted in center comes out clean.

*Green onion and almond milk also make this recipe FODMAP-free. (FODMAPs are foods which contain one or more of these: Fermentable Oligosaccharides, Disaccharides, Monosaccharides, and Polyols.)

PER SERVING: Calories 320; Fat 22.8 g (Saturated 8.6 g); Cholesterol 206 mg; Sodium 617 mg; Carbohydrate 12.4 g; Fiber 1 g; Sugars 1.8 g; Protein 16.9 g

Granola

Violet Wickes, Student Accounts, Controller's Office

Serves 12

3½ cups oats
⅓ cup butter, melted
⅓ cup honey
¼ cup firmly packed brown sugar
1 tsp. vanilla extract
½ cup chopped nuts
1 cup chopped mixed dried fruit

Bake at 350°. In a 15 x 10-in. baking pan, combine all ingredients except fruit; mix well and spread evenly. Bake 20 to 25 minutes, or until golden brown, stirring after 10 minutes. Cool and mix in fruit.

Recipe Continues

PER SERVING: Calories 250; Fat 9.7 g (Saturated 3.9 g); Cholesterol 14 mg; Sodium 80 mg; Carbohydrate 38.8 g; Fiber 4.2 g; Sugars 11.2 g; Protein 4.6 g

Höska

"My sister-in-law and her sister learned how to make this traditional bread from their Bohemian grandmother, and they passed it on to me; now all our daughters make it, and when we're together for Christmas all the grandchildren get involved helping. When we're not all together, we text each other with pictures of our respective Höskas as they come out of the oven."

Judy Groulx, Emeritus Associate Professor, College of Education

Serves 16

2 Tbsp. yeast (1 oz.), bakers' cake yeast, if possible
1¼ cups milk
1 to 2 cups sugar
3 eggs
4 to 5 cups flour
¾ cup butter (1¾ sticks)
1 tsp vanilla

Filling:
1⅓ cups brown sugar, packed
1½ cups walnuts or pecans, chopped small
½ cup (1 stick) butter

Bake at 350°. Crumble yeast into a tall glass, add ¼ cup warm milk and 1 tsp. sugar; set aside to let rise. In a large bowl mix 3 beaten eggs with 1 Tbsp. sugar; gradually add 1 cup boiling milk, beating constantly so eggs don't cook. Add and mix in ½ cup sugar, then add enough flour to make a paste. Add yeast mixture to dough mix. Keep adding flour until dough

Recipe Continues

is stiff (at some point you'll have to switch from using a spoon to using your hands). Melt butter and add to mixture. Knead dough and add flour until mixture does not stick to bowl. Cover bowl with a moist towel and set aside in a warm place; let dough rise to double its size. Mix together the filling ingredients while waiting.

Lay out the dough on a board, using plenty of flour on the board and on a rolling pin. Separate dough into 5 equal parts. One-by-one, make oblongs and roll into strips (about 10 x 3½ in.). Spoon filling onto each strip and close up by pinching dough together at the seam and ends, using a little water to seal. Grease a large roasting pan. With 3 of the rolls, make a braid for the bottom of the bread and place in the pan; twist the other 2 rolls together and lay on top. Let rise again about half an hour. Then bake uncovered for 1 hour.

PER SERVING: Calories 637; Fat 45.3 g (Saturated 24.6 g); Cholesterol 131 mg; Sodium 292 mg; Carbohydrate 52.9 g; Fiber 1.9 g; Sugars 27.4 g; Protein 8.4 g

Not Your Mother's Banana Bread

"My daughter Amy Allen McLain, a 1995 TCU graduate, gave me this recipe, which I make whenever I have ripe bananas. It is a very moist, delicious bread."

Phyllis Allen, Coordinator of the Skills Lab for Harris College of Nursing and Health Sciences

Makes 2 loaves

1 cup shortening (or 2 sticks of butter)
2 cups sugar
6 ripe bananas, mashed
4 eggs

Recipe Continues

2¼ cups flour
1 tsp. salt
2 tsp. baking soda
1 tsp. cinnamon
1 tsp. allspice
½ tsp. ground cloves
½ tsp. nutmeg
1 cup chopped pecans (optional)

Bake at 350°. Cream butter and sugar. Add mashed bananas. Add eggs one at a time, beating with each addition. Add dry ingredients to banana mixture. Spread in two greased 8 x 4-in. loaf pans or several smaller ones. Bake for 45 to 50 minutes.

PER SERVING: Calories 408; Fat 21.2 g (Saturated 5.2 g); Cholesterol 44 mg; Sodium 340 mg; Carbohydrate 53 g; Fiber 2.8 g; Sugars 32.9 g; Protein 4.9 g

Tater Tot Sausage Breakfast Casserole

"My daughter, TCU '04, prepares this for breakfast every Christmas morning."

Joe Ann May, Financial Assistant, Financial Services Department

Serves 8 to 10

2 lbs. hot breakfast sausage
1 (30 to 32-oz.) bag frozen tater tots
1½ cups shredded cheddar cheese
½ cup mozzarella cheese
12 eggs
1 tsp. salt
½ tsp. pepper
¼ tsp. garlic powder

Recipe Continues

¼ tsp. onion powder
2 cups milk

Bake at 350°. In a large skillet, cook sausage until no longer pink. Drain fat. In a large bowl, toss together tater tots, cooked sausage, and cheeses. Pour into a lightly greased 9 x 13-in. pan. Whisk together eggs, salt, pepper, garlic powder, onion powder, and milk. Pour over tater tot mixture. You can cover and refrigerate at this point to bake later. Bake uncovered for 60 to 70 minutes, or until eggs are set.

PER SERVING: Calories 643; Fat 46 g (Saturated 16.3 g); Cholesterol 295 mg; Sodium 1457 mg; Carbohydrate 23.5 g; Fiber 2.1 g; Sugars 3.3 g; Protein 32.6 g

Mary Couts Burnett Library at TCU. TCU Marketing and Communication. *Photo by Amy Peterson.*

SALADS

Cranberry Salad

"This is a traditional family recipe passed down from my mother-in-law, Irene Gilmore, served at Thanksgiving. You can use a food processor, but she used a food and meat grinder. My mother gave me hers, which I use."

Sharon Campbell, Administrative Assistant, AddRan College

Serves 6 to 8

1 lb. fresh cranberries
1 lb. sugar (2 cups)
1 large orange, peeled (reserve ½ of orange peel)
1 large apple, unpeeled
1 (3-oz.) package strawberry Jell-O, dissolved in 1 cup hot water

Grind cranberries, peeled orange and ½ of orange peeling, and apple into a large bowl. Mix in sugar. Add Jell-O and let set.

PER SERVING: Calories 279; Fat 0.1 g (Saturated 0 g); Cholesterol 0 mg; Sodium 11 mg; Carbohydrate 70.8 g; Fiber 3.3 g; Sugars 66.2 g; Protein 0 g

Dublin Salad

"This recipe comes from my mother, Mildred, a wonderful cook. I don't think she ever went to Dublin, but she knew what to do with a cantaloupe. My wife recommends Israeli feta, if you can find it."

Pat Miller, Registrar

Serves 6

1 head of red leaf lettuce
⅔ cup broken walnut pieces

Recipe Continues

½ cup feta cheese
2 cups cantaloupe cubes
¼ cup honey
2 Tbsp. lemon juice
2 Tbsp. lime juice

Combine lettuce, walnuts, feta cheese, and cantaloupe cubes. In a separate container mix honey, lemon juice, and lime juice to make the dressing. Pour over lettuce mixture and toss to coat ingredients with dressing.

PER SERVING: Calories 279; Fat 0.1 g (Saturated 0g); Cholesterol 0 mg; Sodium 19 mg; Carbohydrate 70.7 g; Fiber 3.3 g; Sugars 66.1 g; Protein 0.4 g

Dukes Family Cranberry Salad

"This is a fresh and delicious version of cranberry sauce or relish that my mother always made for Thanksgiving dinner and sometimes at Christmas to accompany roasted turkey. My family loved it (but we also liked the canned cranberry sauce!). This dish is more like a relish and has a fresh, sweet flavor due to the fresh apple, orange, and nuts. I found it very important to grind the cranberries and orange together the day before one plans to prepare the recipe—otherwise, the fruits won't macerate and give the dark red color and deep flavor to the dish. And it is best to grind the fruits, not chop them—it makes for a much better texture and better color and flavor."

Sharon Fairchild, Emeritus Associate Professor of French

Serves 8

2 cups fresh cranberries
1 orange
1 cup sugar

Recipe Continues

1 (3-oz.) package lemon Jell-O
1½ cups boiling water
1 cup chopped apple
1 cup chopped walnuts (or pecans)
1 (8-oz.) can crushed pineapple

Grind together cranberries and the whole orange (including peel). This works best using a food/meat grinder or a food processor. Pour sugar over cranberry mixture, mix and let stand several hours in refrigerator (overnight is best). Dissolve Jell-O in boiling water. Let cool. Mix cooled Jell-O into cranberry mixture, then add apple, nuts, and pineapple. Let set in refrigerator until thickened.

PER SERVING: Calories 285; Fat 9.3 g (Saturated .5 g); Cholesterol 0 mg; Sodium 61 mg; Carbohydrate 48.8 g; Fiber 3.7 g; Sugars 43.5 g; Protein 5.2 g

Japanese-style Dressing

"In 1997, I hosted a Japanese competitor in the Van Cliburn Piano Competition for three weeks. After my guest did not advance past the preliminary stage of the competition, I taught him to drive, and he cooked . . . a great deal for me! He made this delicious salad dressing and wrote down the ingredients for me in longhand."

Janet George Herald, Associate Dean of Admissions

Serves 8

½ cup rice vinegar
½ cup oil
½ cup toasted sesame oil
½ cup soy sauce
¼ cup sugar
salt and pepper

Recipe Continues

onions, diced
dried hot chili pepper flakes

This recipe can be easily adjusted for quantity by combining equal parts of rice vinegar, oil, sesame oil, and soy sauce with ½ part of sugar. Add salt and pepper, diced onions, and hot chili pepper flakes to taste.

Nutritional values are based on using ½ cup for the first four ingredients and ¼ cup of sugar.

PER SERVING: Calories 284; Fat 27.3 g (Saturated 3.7 g); Cholesterol 0 mg; Sodium 899 mg; Carbohydrate 7.8 g; Fiber 0.2 g; Sugars 6.7 g; Protein 1 g

---

Kim's Salad

"I received this salad recipe from my daughter. It is a great salad that will serve several people. Suggested measurements are to serve 6 to 8 people, but quantities may be adjusted to suit your preferences. This dish most often accompanied the entrée, along with one or two other side dishes at my mother's—Esther Winesanker's—dinner parties, but she also made it for special family dinners. It went down so easily, and its sweet and sour flavors always complemented the rest of the meal beautifully."

Joan Yates, Administrative Assistant, International Admissions

Serves 6 to 8

Newman's Own Olive Oil and Vinegar dressing
(enough to dampen greens, about 2 to 3 Tbsp.)
1 large plastic tub spring salad mix
1 pint cherry tomatoes, cut in half
¼ to ½ cup feta cheese crumbles, or to taste
¼ to ½ cup walnuts or almonds, sliced or chopped, or to taste
2 to 3 avocados, cut into squares

Recipe Continues

2 Tbsp. dried cranberries, or to taste

Toss preferred amounts of all of the above ingredients together and serve.

PER SERVING: Calories 251; Fat 9.3 g (Saturated 0.5 g); Cholesterol 0 mg; Sodium 11 mg; Carbohydrate 40.5 g; Fiber 3.3 g; Sugars 35.5 g; Protein 4.3 g

Lime-Pear Mold

"My mother included this dish, which she sometimes doubled or tripled, depending on the size of the party, at most all of the gatherings of the Fine Arts Department faculty at our home. Over the years it was always a favorite of her guests, and, as girls, my sister and I were always delighted if there was any left over."

Miriam Levy, daughter of Michael Winesanker, Professor of Musicology and Chair of the Music Department, and Esther Winesanker, Library

Serves 8

1 (3-oz.) package lime Jell-O
1½ cups boiling water
½ cup juice from canned pears
¼ tsp. salt
1 tsp. white vinegar
2 cups diced pears, drained (large can)
6 oz. cream cheese (1½ 4-oz. blocks of cream cheese)

Dissolve Jell-O in boiling water. Add pear juice. Pour half into greased ring mold.* Place in refrigerator to set. Whip remaining Jell-O and cream cheese in blender until light and frothy. Add vinegar, salt, and diced pears. Pour on top of firmly congealed Jell-O and refrigerate over-

Recipe Continues

night. To determine the size of the mold, figure that you will be using 4+ cups of ingredients, and you don't want to fill it to the top.

*Grease the sides and bottom of mold with margarine. To unmold, carefully lower whole mold (up to the top edge) into hot water, count to 5 slowly, run a knife around edges, place plate over top of mold, and invert quickly onto the plate. If you like, you can decorate the inside of the ring with a flower or purple cabbage.

PER SERVING: Calories 99; Fat 7.4g (Saturated 4.7g); Cholesterol 23 mg; Sodium 152 mg; Carbohydrate 6.7 g; Fiber 0.3 g; Sugars 5.9 g; Protein 1.9 g

Madsen Family Salad

"My mother-in-law used to make this salad for every family gathering, and now I do the same. It's very popular, and people always ask me for the dressing recipe."

Nancy Madsen, Director of Donor Relations

Serves 6 to 8

Salad:
One head or two bags romaine
½ cup or more of freshly grated Romano or Parmesan cheese
Toasted sesame seeds or Tours mix.* Pour enough to cover the bottom of a round cake pan.

Dressing:
½ cup salad or tarragon vinegar
1½ cups salad oil
McCormick Salad Supreme seasoning mix

Recipe Continues

For the dressing, combine vinegar, oil, and seasoning mix in a jar with a tight lid; shake well. This may be prepared and refrigerated up to several days ahead.

For the salad, tear lettuce into bite-size pieces and toss with cheese and sesame seeds or Tours mix. Toss with dressing right before serving.

*Tours mix can be purchased at Vending Nut Company off Montgomery Street. Sometimes I don't toast the seeds/nuts. You can buy already toasted sesame seeds, but they are more expensive.

PER SERVING: Calories 452; Fat 48.9 g (Saturated 7.7 g); Cholesterol 3 mg; Sodium 49 mg; Carbohydrate 2.2 g; Fiber 0.6 g; Sugars 0.5 g; Protein 1.8 g

Make-Ahead Leaf Lettuce Salad

"It's my favorite go-to salad. It was brought to our TCU football tailgate by my coworker Pam James in the Financial Services department."

Joe Ann May, Financial Assistant, Financial Services Department

Serves 6

½ cup oil (canola or olive)
8 green onions including tops, chopped
2 avocados, sliced
1 Tbsp. Accent
1 Tbsp. seasoned salt
juice of 2 fresh lemons (3 Tbsp. lemon juice)
1 head leaf lettuce (red or green), chopped
1 head leafy romaine lettuce, chopped
shredded Parmesan cheese

Recipe Continues

In the order listed, place ½ cup oil, then onions, avocados, Accent, salt, and lemon juice in the bottom of a deep salad bowl. Do not mix. Alternate on top, half of the one head of chopped leaf lettuce (green or red tip), and one head of chopped leafy romaine lettuce. Cover with plastic wrap and store in refrigerator overnight. Just before serving, sprinkle with shredded Parmesan cheese. Toss well when ready to serve.

PER SERVING: Calories 306; Fat 31.3 g (Saturated 5.2 g); Cholesterol 0 mg; Sodium 769 mg; Carbohydrate 7.4 g; Fiber 5 g; Sugars 1 g; Protein 1.7 g

Mango Salad

"This recipe came from a dear friend of my mother's. When I made it for the first time, my family loved it, especially my nephew and youngest daughter. It's not a typical Jell-O salad, and my family probably like it because it is creamy and a bit sweet. It appears very often on my table!"

Nancy Madsen, Director of Donor Relations

Serves 8

3 (3-oz.) packages lemon Jell-O
3 cups boiling water
1 (16-oz.) can (or jar) mangos
1 (8-oz.) cream cheese at room temperature
1 cup mango juice (from above can or jar)

Pour water over Jell-O in large bowl. Stir to dissolve—about 2 minutes. Drain mangos into measuring cup to get one cup of juice. If you can't get one cup, add water to make one cup. In blender or food processor, combine cream cheese and mangos; slowly pour in the cup of juice. Pour the cream cheese-mango mixture into the Jell-O that has been cooled and stir well. Pour mixture into a 2½ quart mold or glass dish and chill to jell.

Recipe Continues

PER SERVING: Calories 254; Fat 9.9 g (Saturated 6.2 g); Cholesterol 31 mg; Sodium 264 mg; Carbohydrate 38.2 g; Fiber 0.5 g; Sugars 37 g; Protein 5.1 g

Oriental Salad

"This Oriental Salad recipe was given to me by Leah Flowers, who got it from Nancy Cook. (Leah was fastidious about giving credit to her source of information.) Leah took this salad to a Christmas Party for Chancel Choir members at University Christian Church. It became a Chancel Choir Christmas Party favorite. It also could be called Fusion Oriental Salad, I think, because it combines a variety of ingredients to create a festival of flavor."

Maggie Thomas, Emeritus Professor of Journalism

Serves 8

Salad:
1 16-oz. package coleslaw mix
Add some shredded purple cabbage and torn-up leaf lettuce
(Add one 9-oz. package torn Romaine lettuce to make a larger salad.)
½ to 1 cup shelled sunflower seeds
½ to 1 cup toasted almond slivers
2 packages chicken ramen noodles
1 small can mandarin orange slices

Dressing:
1 cup oil
½ cup sugar
⅓ cup white vinegar
seasoning packets from both packages of chicken ramen noodles

Recipe Continues

Mix all but noodles and mandarin oranges and refrigerate. Just before serving, break up ramen noodles, add to salad, add dressing, and mix well. Top with orange slices.

PER SERVING: Calories 308; Fat 18.2 g (Saturated 4.1 g); Cholesterol 0 mg; Sodium 800 mg; Carbohydrate 30.6 g; Fiber 2.4 g; Sugars 5.9 g; Protein 7.8 g

Pasta Salad

"I have been traveling on a girls' trip with my two daughters and their friends for ten years now. We usually go to Fredericksburg but have also stayed closer to home a couple of years. I always make this salad to eat with a picnic lunch at one of the wineries we visit."

Nancy Madsen, Director of Donor Relations

Serves 10

Dressing:
¼ cup freshly squeezed lemon juice (about 2 medium lemons)
½ cup white balsamic vinegar (another kind of balsamic is okay)
2 tablespoons honey
⅔ cup extra virgin olive oil
Kosher salt and freshly ground black pepper
1 cup feta cheese, crumbled

Make the dressing first. In a bowl, whisk together the lemon juice, vinegar, honey, and olive oil; season with salt and pepper. Whisk in the feta cheese; cover and refrigerate until ready to use.

Recipe Continues

Salad:
1 lb. orzo pasta, uncooked
1 (16-oz.) bag baby greens, spinach, arugula, and/or romaine
5 green onions, white and green parts, thinly sliced
1 cup cherry tomatoes, halved
½ cup feta cheese, crumbled
1 Tbsp. dried oregano
¼ cup pine nuts
Kalamata olives and sliced cucumbers, if desired

In a large pot, cook the orzo in salted water according to package directions. Drain and run cold water over the pasta to stop the cooking. Put the orzo in a large bowl and toss with ½ cup of the dressing. Add the green onions and tomatoes and, if using, olives and cucumbers (I don't use them), feta cheese, and oregano. Add dressing and toss well. Sometimes I omit the feta cheese in the dressing and just add it to the salad. This makes a lot of salad.

PER SERVING: Calories 467; Fat 28.2 g (Saturated 7.5 g); Cholesterol 66 mg; Sodium 848 mg; Carbohydrate 41.4 g; Fiber 1.9 g; Sugars 7.3 g; Protein 14.6 g

Pretzel Jell-O Salad

"This is a family favorite from my mother. My sons insist on it at any family dinner."

DeVonna Tinney, Director of Development, Harris College of Nursing and Health Sciences

Serves 8 to 12

Recipe Continues

Crust:
2 cups unsalted chopped pretzels
¾ cup melted butter
3 Tbsp. sugar

Filling:
1 cup sugar
8 oz. cream cheese
8 oz. Cool Whip
1 large (6-oz.) package strawberry Jell-O
2 cups hot water
10 oz. frozen strawberries

Bake at 350°. Combine pretzels, butter, and 3 Tbsp. sugar. Press into 9 x 12-in. pan and bake for 8 minutes. Cool completely. To make the filling mix cream cheese and sugar. Fold in Cool Whip and spread on crust. Mix package of strawberry Jell-O with 2 cups of hot water and add frozen strawberries while still frozen. Put on top of cream cheese mixture and cool.

PER SERVING: Calories 421; Fat 22.5 g (Saturated 13.9 g); Cholesterol 62 mg; Sodium 249 mg; Carbohydrate 53.4 g; Fiber 1.2 g; Sugars 34.5 g; Protein 4.1 g

Horned Frog Statue. *Photo by Jane Mackay.*

SOUPS

Barley Beef Soup

"My aunt Jean introduced me to barley beef soup. Over the years I started roasting the beef, mushrooms, and shallots together and liked how the recipe evolved. It's a nice hearty winter soup."

Cecilia Silva, Professor of Education

Serves 6 to 8

2 lb. lean sirloin, cut into ½-inch cubes
2 lb. mushrooms, quartered
1 shallot, chopped
2 Tbsp. olive oil
Salt and pepper, to taste
3 cloves garlic, minced
1 onion, chopped
1 cup celery, chopped
1 cup carrots, sliced
6 cups beef broth
1 cup barley, soaked overnight
1 bay leaf
¼ tsp. marjoram
¼ tsp. thyme

Bake at 425°. In a roasting pan or rimmed baking sheet, toss beef, mushrooms, shallot, and olive oil. Season with salt and pepper. Arrange in a single layer. Roast until browned, about 30 minutes. In the soup pot brown garlic; add onions and cook until soft. Add herbs, celery, carrots, and broth to the pot. Simmer about 20 minutes until celery and carrots are tender. Puree this vegetable mix. Return to soup pot and add barley, meat, and mushrooms. Simmer 1 hour.

PER SERVING: Calories 537; Fat 18.3 g (Saturated 4.9 g); Cholesterol 88 mg; Sodium 1290 mg; Carbohydrate 33.3 g; Fiber 8 g; Sugars 6.5 g; Protein 60.2 g

Crockpot French Onion Soup

Karen Stone, Director, Brown-Lupton Gallery and spouse of
Howard Stone, Professor of Pastoral Theology, Brite School of Divinity

Serves 6 generously, or 10 as a first course

3 Tbsp. unsalted butter, cut into 3 pieces
5 lb. yellow onions, cut pole to pole in ¼ in. slices (do not use sweet onions)
½ tsp. salt (more if using homemade beef broth, less if using "Better than Bouillon")
2½ cups water, plus extra for deglazing
⅔ to ¾ cup dry sherry
5 cups low-sodium chicken broth
2½ cups beef broth or 2½ cups water + 2½ tsp. beef flavor "Better than Bouillon," low sodium
8 sprigs fresh thyme, tied with kitchen string
2 bay leaves
black pepper
1 small baguette, cut on bias into ½ inch slices
8 oz. Gruyere or Comte cheese, shredded (about 2½ cups)

In the morning:
Spray slow cooker with nonstick coating or insert crockpot liner; set on high. Put butter in pot and add onions and 1 tsp. salt. Do not add liquid. Cook on high for 6 to 8 hours, stirring occasionally, until onions are completely soft and caramelized but not melted. Reduce heat to low if they are cooking too quickly, as slow cookers vary.

Late afternoon, or when onions are ready:
Transfer onions to heavy Dutch oven and place on top of stove at medium-high heat. Cook onions, stirring frequently and scraping bottom and sides of pot, until liquid evaporates and onions brown, 15 to 20 minutes, reducing heat to medium if onions start to burn. Continue to cook, stirring frequently, until bottom of pot is coated with a dark crust, 6 to 8 minutes, adjusting heat as necessary. Stir in ¼ cup water, scrape crust

Recipe Continues

off bottom, and cook 6 to 8 min. until water evaporates and another dark crust has formed. Repeat three or four more times, until onions are very dark brown but not burned. Stir in sherry and cook, stirring until sherry evaporates, about 5 minutes. Stir in broths, water, thyme, bay leaf, and salt, scraping remaining crust. Increase heat to high, then to simmer. Cover and simmer approximately 30 minutes. Remove and discard herbs, then season to taste with salt and pepper.

Prepare croutons:
Bake at 400°. While soup simmers, spread baguette slices on rimmed baking sheet and bake until dry, crisp, and golden.

Serve:
Adjust oven rack 6 inches from broiler and heat broiler. Put broiler-safe bowls on baking sheet and distribute soup evenly. (You may have left-over soup: Yay!) Top each bowl with 1 or 2 pieces of toasted bread side-by-side, and spread with cheese. Broil until cheese is melted, 3 to 5 minutes (watch carefully). Let cool 5 minutes before serving.

PER SERVING: Calories 735; Fat 22.5 g (Saturated 12 g); Cholesterol 57 mg; Sodium 2455 mg; Carbohydrate 92.3 g; Fiber 10.4 g; Sugars 19.9 g; Protein 37 g

Elaine's Minestrone

"I was introduced to this recipe by a good friend when we lived in California. Elaine lived in San Francisco, and when we would drive from Los Angeles, she would always have a pot of Minestrone on the stove, ready for us. Didn't matter what time we arrived, a bowl of soup and a piece of bread would always taste delicious. Became one of our family favorites over the years."

Cecilia Silva, Professor of Education

Recipe Continues

Serves 8 to 10

½ cup dried white beans
4 Tbsp. (½ stick) butter
1 cup green peas
1 cup diced zucchini (about 1 large zucchini)
1 cup diced carrots (about 2 carrots)
⅓ cup sliced celery (about 1 stalk)
2 large red potatoes, diced
2 oz. salt pork
2 Tbsp. chopped onion
½ cup chopped leeks (about 1 leek)
2 cups chopped tomatoes (about 6 to 8 Roma tomatoes)
2 quarts chicken stock
1 bay leaf
½ cup rice or small pasta such as orzo

Garnish:
parsley snips
grated Parmesan cheese

Soak the beans overnight; drain. Bring 1 quart water to a boil. Add the beans and simmer for two hours. Set aside. Melt the butter, then add peas, zucchini, carrots, celery, and potatoes. Cook 3 to 5 minutes. Fry the salt pork, onion, and leeks. Stir in the tomatoes, vegetables, chicken stock, and onion mix. Add bay leaf. Bring to a boil and simmer for 25 minutes. Add rice and beans. Simmer 25 more minutes. Garnish with parsley and cheese.

PER SERVING: Calories 290; Fat 11.6 g (Saturated 5.6 g); Cholesterol 21 mg; Sodium 833 mg; Carbohydrate 39.6 g; Fiber 5.8 g; Sugars 5.4 g; Protein 8.7 g

Lady-Lunch Tomato Soup

"Tea rooms were an important gathering spot for women in the South in the days when many women were confined to the home. The menu featured dainty dishes such as finger sandwiches, chicken salad with grapes, and little cups of soup. I can remember many 'lady lunches' with my mother, grandmothers, and aunts; in my earliest memories, I wore gloves and Mary Janes. These days, there aren't many tea rooms left, but I still like to make some of their dishes, including this soup, which was always served in demitasse cups."

Bonnie Frederick, Emeritus Professor of Modern Languages

Serves 6

4 cups low-sodium chicken broth
4 cups tomato juice
1 cup chopped green onions
2 tsp. tomato paste
½ tsp. each: thyme, basil, allspice, sugar
2 tsp. lemon juice
2 Tbsp. dry sherry

Simmer first 4 ingredients plus seasonings gently for 15 minutes: Strain out the onions. The soup can be refrigerated at this point. When ready to serve, add lemon juice and sherry and heat.

PER SERVING: Calories 134; Fat 0.1 g (Saturated 0 g); Cholesterol 0 mg; Sodium 814 mg; Carbohydrate 14 g; Fiber 1.2 g; Sugars 6.4 g; Protein 12.3 g

Mom's Leek Soup

"The thing about leek soup is that other than at home, you can't find it in many places. This is one of the recipes I asked my mother to make every time we got together—didn't matter where we were. I remember being in Spain one summer where she made the soup—much to the dismay of friends and family, who wouldn't consider having hot soup during warm weather."

Cecilia Silva, Professor of Education

Serves 6

2 leeks, rinsed carefully and sliced
1 onion, chopped
2 Tbsp. butter
3 cups chicken broth
2 potatoes, sliced
1 (12-oz.) can evaporated milk
Chopped parsley for garnish

Sauté the leeks and onion in butter until soft. Add chicken broth and sliced potatoes. Cook until the potatoes are done. Add the evaporated milk. Garnish with chopped parsley.

PER SERVING: Calories 210; Fat 9.4 g (Saturated 5.5 g); Cholesterol 28 mg; Sodium 485 mg; Carbohydrate 23.7 g; Fiber 2.6 g; Sugars 9.3 g; Protein 8.5 g

Navy Bean Soup

Spencer Wertz, Emeritus Professor of Philosophy

Serves 4 to 6

½ to 1 lb. navy beans
1 onion cut in half (take out at the end of cooking)
1 sprig of fresh rosemary (take out at the end of cooking)
4 cloves of minced garlic
1 ham hock (smoked), cut up if possible
2 cups chicken broth
2½ cups water
1 Tbsp. sea salt
1 pinch of red chili flakes
salt to taste
black pepper to taste
parsley for garnish (if desired)

Rinse and sort beans; soak according to package directions. Drain and rinse, discarding liquid. Place in a Dutch oven. Add remaining ingredients, including sea salt but not table salt or black pepper. Bring to a boil. Reduce heat; cover and simmer until beans are tender, about 1½ hours. Add more water if necessary. Add salt and black pepper to taste when beans are nearly done. Remove ham hock and let stand until cool enough to handle. Remove meat from bone; discard bone. Cut meat into bite-sized pieces; set aside. (For a thicker soup, cool slightly, then puree beans in a food processor or blender and return to pot.) Return ham to soup and heat through. Garnish with parsley

PER SERVING: Calories 397; Fat 18.4 g (Saturated 6.9 g); Cholesterol 80 mg; Sodium 327 mg; Carbohydrate 25.6 g; Fiber 9.7 g; Sugars 2.5 g; Protein 31.1 g

Sunday Supper Soup

"This is one of my family's favorite recipes. You can use frozen meatballs, but they're not nearly as good, in my opinion."

Nancy Madsen, Director of Donor Relations

Makes 6 servings, about 2 quarts

Meatballs:
1½ lb. ground beef (the leaner the better)
1 egg, slightly beaten
½ cup soft bread crumbs
¼ tsp. salt
1 Tbsp. chopped parsley (the dried kind is fine)

Soup:
3 Tbsp. + 2 cups water
2 Tbsp. butter or margarine
1 (10.5-oz.) can beef broth, more if desired
1 (10.5-oz.) can tomatoes, undrained
1 envelope dry onion soup mix
2 cups (4 or 5) pared sliced carrots
¼ cup chopped celery tops
¼ cup chopped parsley
¼ tsp. pepper
¼ tsp. dried oregano
¼ tsp. dried basil
1 bay leaf

In a medium bowl, combine beef, egg, 3 tablespoons water, bread crumbs, salt, and parsley; mix lightly. With hands, lightly shape into balls (about 24). In hot butter, sauté meatballs, a single layer at a time, until browned on all sides. Drain off fat and set aside. In same pan, combine 2 cups water, broth, tomatoes, onion soup mix, carrots, celery tops, parsley, pepper, oregano, basil, and bay leaf. Bring to a boil, then cover, reduce

Recipe Continues

heat, and simmer for 30 minutes, stirring occasionally. Add meatballs and simmer 20 minutes longer. Garnish with chopped parsley, if desired.

PER SERVING: Calories 350; Fat 11.7 g (Saturated 5.2 g); Cholesterol 112 mg; Sodium 1908 mg; Carbohydrate 22 g; Fiber 2.7 g; Sugars 13.6 g; Protein 38.2 g

Taco Soup

"I received the Taco Soup recipe from Marsha Williams (she worked in Admissions in the 80s and 90s). It is a favorite of ours in winter—I always freeze half of it, so it is easy to pull out of the freezer on cold days!"

Wendy Crowley, Director of Student Financial Services

Serves 8

1 lb. ground meat (can use ground turkey)
½ cup finely chopped onion
1 package taco seasoning
1 package dry ranch dressing
1 (14.5-oz.) can diced tomatoes with jalapeños (not Rotel), undrained
1 (16-oz.) can tomato sauce
1 (10-oz.) can Rotel tomatoes, undrained
2 (16-oz.) cans pinto beans, undrained
1 (15.25-oz.) can corn, undrained
1 (approximately 15-oz.) can water
grated cheese, if desired
sliced avocados, if desired

Brown meat with onions. Add all other ingredients, and simmer for 30 minutes. Top with grated cheese and sliced avocados, if desired. Serve with chips.

Recipe Continues

PER SERVING: Calories 538; Fat 5.8 g (Saturated 2.2 g); Cholesterol 47 mg; Sodium 436 mg; Carbohydrate 80.4 g; Fiber 19.4 g; Sugars 7.3 g; Protein 41.5 g

Frog Fountain in the snow. TCU Marketing and Communication.
Photo by Glen E. Ellman.

SIDE DISHES

Asparagus Casserole

"This is a family favorite from my mother. My sons insist on it at any family dinner."

DeVonna Tinney, Director of Development, Harris College of Nursing and Health Sciences

Serves 4 to 5

4 Tbsp. (½ stick) melted butter
1 cup Hellmann's mayonnaise
½ tsp. salt
¼ tsp. pepper
¼ tsp. dry mustard
Juice of one lemon
2 (15-oz.) cans of asparagus (I use Green Giant spears; the ones in the silver can are too thick.)
Parmesan cheese
10 to 12 crushed club crackers

Bake at 350°. Mix melted butter, mayonnaise, salt, pepper, mustard, and lemon juice. Place drained asparagus in the bottom of a dish and pour mixture over. Sprinkle ½ to 1 cup of Parmesan cheese over top. Crush 10 to 12 club crackers and scatter on top. Bake for 20 minutes or until bubbly.

PER SERVING: Calories 342; Fat 26.3 g (Saturated 8 g); Cholesterol 30 mg; Sodium 870 mg; Carbohydrate 19.4 g; Fiber 1.6 g; Sugars 3 g; Protein 9 g

Birthday Potato Casserole

"This is my son's favorite dish. It is always served on his birthday with steak, roasted asparagus, and salad."

Wendy Crowley, Director of Student Financial Services

Serves 10 to 12

2 lb. bag frozen hashed brown potatoes
2 cups grated Velveeta cheese
1 (10.5-oz.) can cream of chicken soup
1 pint sour cream
3 Tbsp. finely grated onion
salt and pepper to taste
corn flakes (optional)

Bake at 300°. Butter sides and bottom of 9 x 13-in. pan. Partially thaw potatoes. In a large bowl, combine potatoes, cheese, soup, sour cream, and onions. Salt and pepper to taste and mix well. Top with corn flakes, if desired (I omit this step). Bake for 1 hour.

PER SERVING: Calories 274; Fat 20.1 g (Saturated 10.8 g); Cholesterol 43 mg; Sodium 728 mg; Carbohydrate 17 g; Fiber .7 g; Sugars 3.5 g; Protein 9.4 g

Chop Chop Potatoes

"My Aunt Elizabeth made this variation of scalloped potatoes for every family holiday dinner. It is described by a niece as 'a recipe of almost mythical proportions.'"

Cynthia Chapa, Department of Modern Languages

Recipe Continues

Serves 6 to 8

6 large potatoes (any variety)
½ cup flour
1 cup (2 sticks) butter
½ pint half and half (or evaporated milk or heavy cream)
salt to taste

Bake at 350°. Wash and boil potatoes until done (a bit on the hard side). Peel and allow to cool. Sprinkle cutting board and potatoes with flour. Chop potatoes a few at a time (with serrated hand food chopper) and sprinkle with flour and a small amount of salt. Chop quite fine. Spray casserole dish with cooking spray. Place a layer of chopped potatoes, sprinkle lightly with flour and dot with small pieces of butter. Repeat until casserole is full, using about 1 stick of butter in all. No flour on the top layer. Heat half and half (or milk or cream) and the other stick of butter and pour over potatoes. Cover and bake 1 hour. Remove cover and bake 30 additional minutes.

PER SERVING: Calories 461; Fat 26.7 g (Saturated 16.7 g); Cholesterol 72 mg; Sodium 211 mg; Carbohydrate 50.8 g; Fiber 6.9 g; Sugars 3.3 g; Protein 6.6 g

Corn Casserole

"Even though this recipe is now known by heart, I fondly remember taking it to the fun tailgate parties and lunches we shared together in the TCU Office of Admission. Good food and fun times make happy employees, and this dish always delivered!"

Kathryn Schruba, Coordinator of Admission Office Services

Recipe Continues

Serves 6 to 8

½ cup (1 stick) butter
1 (15-oz.) can whole kernel corn, drained
1 (15-oz.) can creamed corn
1 pint sour cream
1 small box corn muffin mix

Bake at 350 °. Melt butter in 9 x 13-in. casserole dish. Drain butter into glass bowl. Combine butter, whole kernel corn, and creamed corn. Add sour cream; mix well. Add corn muffin mix and pour mixture into the casserole dish. Bake 1 hour.

PER SERVING: Calories 358; Fat 24.2 g (Saturated 14.2 g); Cholesterol 52 mg; Sodium 519 mg; Carbohydrate 33.5 g; Fiber 1.9 g; Sugars 8.3 g; Protein 4.6 g

Cornbread Dressing

"The first time we made this dressing was when we were graduate students at the University of Minnesota. Gail, who worked in the pediatrics unit at the University of Minneapolis Hospitals, had volunteered to work on Thanksgiving Day so that her colleagues with children could be with their families. Jack decided to make dressing and called his mother in Texas to get the recipe and the instructions, as we always loved the dressing that she served, and we had never attempted to make dressing before. Being a wonderful cook, she rarely followed a recipe, so she began, as she did with almost any recipe she gave you, by saying, 'For my pan,' you put this amount of this and this amount of that. Jack quickly explained that he did not have her pan, and that he was in Minneapolis and she was in deep East Texas. With that established, she told him the proportions of the various ingredients. With those instructions, as loose as they were, he proceeded to make dressing for Thanksgiving dinner. It turned out well, although

Recipe Continues

we had more dressing than two people could ever have eaten. We have continued to make this recipe over the ensuing fifty-plus years, tweaking the proportions of the ingredients and making a few modifications along the way. We have also learned to reduce the size of the recipe, although it is hard to make dressing except by the tub full."

Gail Davis, Emeritus Professor of Nursing

Serves 12

2½ recipes cornbread (see below), cooled and crumbled
6 cups dried white bread crumbs
3 heaping cups chopped celery
3 heaping cups chopped white onion
3 heaping cups sliced fresh mushrooms
2 to 3 quarts chicken broth
1 cup (2 sticks) butter
salt and pepper to taste
poultry seasoning to taste
rubbed sage to taste
6 eggs
butter for greasing pans

Cornbread:
2 cups yellow cornmeal
2 cups buttermilk
2 eggs
1 teaspoon salt
1 teaspoon baking soda

Cornbread:
Bake at 425°. Mix all ingredients. Pour 3 to 4 tablespoons of oil in a cast iron skillet and heat until it begins to bubble (Don't overheat, as it will catch on fire). Remove from the stove and pour mixture into the hot grease—it should sizzle. Place in the oven and bake until firm—about 20 to 30 minutes. Turn the baked cornbread out onto a cutting board and let cool, then crumble into small pieces.

Recipe Continues

For the dressing:
Bake at 450°. Put crumbled cornbread and dried bread crumbs into a large bowl. Sauté the celery, onion, and mushrooms in the butter. Add vegetable mixture to the crumbs and mix well. Add enough broth to make a soupy mixture. It should run off a spoon easily. (Not having the dressing moist enough will result in the dressing being too dry when cooked.) Add seasonings (too little will result in a bland dressing, while too much can be overpowering). Break the eggs into a separate bowl and whisk lightly, then add to the dressing mixture. Bake uncovered for 30 to 45 minutes, until brown on top.

PER SERVING: Calories 555; Fat 24.8 g (Saturated 12.1 g); Cholesterol 141 mg; Sodium 1377 mg; Carbohydrate 65.3 g; Fiber 3.9 g; Sugars 6.3 g; Protein 17.7 g

Cranberry Chutney

"This recipe was included in our neighborhood newsletter several years ago. The original recipe called for 1 cup of golden raisins, but I do not include those in my chutney. It is now a staple at our Thanksgiving and Christmas gatherings."

Wendy Crowley, Director of Student Financial Services

Serves 24

2 cups Turbinado sugar
2 cups water
4 cups fresh cranberries
Juice of one orange
2 large green apples, peeled and chopped
1 cup chopped pecans
1½ Tbsp. cider vinegar
2 Tbsp. brown sugar

Recipe Continues

½ tsp. cardamom spice
½ tsp. nutmeg
½ tsp. cinnamon

Combine sugar and water in a large saucepan. Bring to a boil, stirring constantly, until sugar dissolves. Reduce heat and add the remaining ingredients. Cook uncovered until berries burst and mixture thickens, stirring occasionally. Remove from heat and let the mixture cool. Refrigerate at least one hour before serving. You can make this a day or two ahead. It will last about a week in the refrigerator.

PER SERVING: Calories 77; Fat 1 g (Saturated 0.1 g); Cholesterol 0 mg; Sodium 1 mg; Carbohydrate 18.3 g; Fiber 1.3 g; Sugars 16.3 g; Protein 0.2 g

Cranberry Salsa

"This is always a great hit at tailgates since there is nothing to spoil. Perfect for Christmas parties, as it has a festive color and can be used as a relish for dinner."

Joe Ann May, Financial Assistant, Financial Services Department

Serves 6 to 8

1 (12-oz.) bag of cranberries, fresh or frozen
1 bunch cilantro, chopped
1 bunch green onions, cut into 3-inch lengths, green tops included
2 jalapeño peppers, seeded and minced (adjust for desired heat)
2 limes, juiced
¼ to ½ cup white sugar (adjust for desired sweetness)
1 pinch salt

Recipe Continues

Chop cranberries first. Next place cilantro, green onions, jalapeño peppers, lime juice, sugar, and salt in food processor and chop to medium consistency; then combine cranberries with cilantro mix. Serve at room temperature with tortilla chips, or over cream cheese with crackers. Makes about 2 cups.

Substitions: Purple onion may be used instead of green; instead of fresh lime use 2 tablespoons bottled lime juice.

PER SERVING: Calories 140; Fat 0.1 g (Saturated 0 g); Cholesterol 0 mg; Sodium 152 mg; Carbohydrate 35.3 g; Fiber 1.6 g; Sugars 31.7 g; Protein 0.4 g

Farmer Boy Apples 'n Onions

"As we were reading Laura Ingalls Wilder's Farmer Boy to our small daughter in the late 1960s, she was intrigued by the frequent mention of 'apples and onions'—apparently a favorite dish at the Wilder household. Patt went to her laboratory (i.e., the kitchen), thought about the ingredients, and came up with this recipe. It's been a family favorite for forty-plus years."

Patt Erisman and Fred Erisman, Emeritus Professor of English

Serves 2 to 3

2 medium sweet onions
2 to 3 medium cooking apples
1 Tbsp. canola oil
3 tsp. mixture of cinnamon and sugar, or more to taste

Peel and slice onions. Heat oil in a sauté pan with a lid. Add onions to pan; cover and cook onions over medium heat, letting them brown. Add small amounts of water as pan gets dry. While onions brown, quarter apples, remove cores, and slice thinly. When onions are well browned,

Recipe Continues

layer apples on top and sprinkle with cinnamon-sugar mixture to taste. Stir together, cover, lower heat, and let simmer until apples are soft. Serve hot.

PER SERVING: Calories 164; Fat 5 g (Saturated 0.3 g); Cholesterol 0 mg; Sodium 4 mg; Carbohydrate 31.6 g; Fiber 5.2 g; Sugars 22.8 g; Protein 1.2 g

Green Bean Swiss Casserole

"This is one of those recipes that came from a good friend on a football afternoon, and it is better than most green bean casseroles—no cream of mushroom soup! It makes football wonderful and goes with any meal."

Linda Moore, Emeritus Professor of Social Work

Serves 5 to 6

1 Tbsp. butter
1 Tbsp. flour
½ tsp. pepper
¼ cup milk
¼ cup chopped onion
½ cup sour cream
1 (15-oz.) can or 2 cups fresh green beans
1½ cups shredded Swiss cheese
⅓ cup bread crumbs

Bake at 400°. Melt butter. Blend in flour and pepper and cook until bubbly. Gradually blend in milk. Remove from heat, add onion and sour cream. Combine sauce with green beans and Swiss cheese and place in a casserole pan. Top with bread crumbs. Bake for 20 minutes.

PER SERVING: Calories 196; Fat 13.8 g (Saturated 8.5 g); Cholesterol 37 mg; Sodium 205 mg; Carbohydrate 10.1 g; Fiber 0.8 g; Sugars 1.7 g; Protein 8.3 g

Green Rice

"This green rice recipe came from one of the very early families in Laredo, Texas. It wasn't a special occasion, but they decided I needed to learn how to cook some Mexican food. They chose this dish because it is easy to prepare and is perfect with fajitas. Enjoy."

Jane Mackay, Emeritus Associate Professor of Information Systems, Neeley School

Serves 10 to 12

2 poblano peppers
1 green bell pepper
½ cup (1 stick) butter or margarine
2 cups sour cream
3 cups Monterey jack cheese, grated
1 cup cooked rice

Bake at 325°. Remove seeds from poblano and bell peppers. Dice into small pieces and sauté in butter or margarine until tender. Put into a blender with sour cream and puree until mixture is smooth. In a bowl, blend together sour cream mix, cheese, and rice. Pour into a 9 x 9-in. greased casserole pan. Bake for 20 to 25 minutes or until bubbly. This is a great make-ahead recipe. You can freeze this cooked and then warm it in the oven or freeze it uncooked and bake it when thawed.

This recipe can be made spicier with a hotter pepper. If you prefer you can also layer the ingredients of pepper mixture, rice, and cheese.

PER SERVING: Calories 380; Fat 29.2 g (Saturated 18.2 g); Cholesterol 75 mg; Sodium 273 mg; Carbohydrate 18.7 g; Fiber 0.5 g; Sugars 1.3 g; Protein 11.5 g

Hash Brown Casserole

"This casserole is an easy way to make a substantial contribution to a meal. The recipe came from Dr. Harriet B. Harral, my Baylor roommate all four years I was there. Harriet's recipe is one her mother and aunt enjoyed serving at family gatherings. Harriet gave me this recipe many years ago when our families went on vacation together."

Maggie Thomas, Emeritus Professor of Journalism

Serves 12

2-lb. bag hash brown Ore Ida potatoes, thawed
½ cup (1 stick) melted butter
½ cup grated onion
1 (10.5-oz.) can cream of chicken soup
1 pint sour cream
2 cups grated American sharp cheese
2 cups crushed cornflakes mixed with ½ cup melted butter

Bake at 350°. Pour all ingredients except for cornflakes into a buttered 3-quart or 9 x 13-in. dish. Cover with corn flakes mixed with butter. Bake for 45 minutes to 1 hour.

PER SERVING: Calories 362; Fat 29.6 g (Saturated 18.3 g); Cholesterol 73 mg; Sodium 598 mg; Carbohydrate 17.9 g; Fiber 1.4 g; Sugars 1.5 g; Protein 7.3 g

Maple Roasted Vegetables

"Our daughter normally dislikes Brussels sprouts, perhaps a side effect of having them during her growing years. This recipe adds some flavor to the usual sprouts so she will eat some of these healthy vegetables. Our dinner guests also like the taste and texture of the vegetables, including the added yellow squash, which fit nicely with a variety of meat or fish entrees."

Carolyn Spence Cagle, Emeritus Professor of Nursing

Serves 4

2 Tbsp. olive oil
1 Tbsp. pure maple syrup
½ tsp. salt
½ tsp. turmeric
½ tsp. black pepper
12 oz. Brussels sprouts, cut in half
8 oz. fresh small carrots

Bake at 450°. Use a whisk to mix olive oil, maple syrup, salt, turmeric, and black pepper. Cover Brussels sprouts and carrots with the mixture and toss to coat. Spread vegetables evenly on a baking sheet lined with aluminum foil, then lightly sprayed with olive oil. Roast until tender (about 20 minutes).

PER SERVING: Calories 119; Fat 7.3 g (Saturated 1.1 g); Cholesterol 0 mg; Sodium 319 mg; Carbohydrate 12.9 g; Fiber 3.8 g; Sugars 5.6 g; Protein 3.2 g

Marinated Tomatoes

"In Spain on a hot day we pulled into a little town, went to the only café on the plaza, and ordered cold food. This salad was part of a platter of cold marinated trout and potato salad. I convinced the cook to show me how to prepare it by promising not to share the recipe with anyone in Spain."

Bonnie Frederick, Emeritus Professor of Modern Languages

Serves 8

3 baskets or string bags of cherry (not grape) tomatoes, halved
6 to 8 green onions, chopped fine (both white and green parts)
3 to 4 Tbsp. cilantro, chopped
¼ cup red wine vinegar
2 Tbsp. olive oil
1 tsp. salt
1 tsp. dried oregano
½ tsp. black pepper

Combine all ingredients and chill 2 hours.

PER SERVING: Calories 78; Fat 3.6 g (Saturated .5 g); Cholesterol 0 mg; Sodium 318 mg; Carbohydrate 10.8 g; Fiber 2.4 g; Sugars 6 g; Protein 2.2 g

Mildred's Baked Beans

"My mother brought this recipe to my fiftieth birthday party. It was a huge hit and became a favorite of many of my friends."

Pat Miller, Registrar

Recipe Continues

Serves 6

1 lb. ground beef
½ cup onion, chopped or sliced
1 green pepper, chopped
½ tsp. salt
¼ tsp. pepper
1 (12-oz.) can pork and beans, drained
½ cup ketchup
1 Tbsp. Worcestershire sauce
1 Tbsp. vinegar
½ tsp. Tabasco

Bake at 350°. Brown together beef, onions, and green pepper. Pour off fat. Add remaining ingredients; mix well. Pour into 1½ quart casserole dish. Bake for 30 minutes.

PER SERVING: Calories 242; Fat 5.3 g (Saturated 1.8 g); Cholesterol 68 mg; Sodium 738 mg; Carbohydrate 20.8 g; Fiber 5.2 g; Sugars 8.1 g; Protein 27.6 g

Tomato Marmalade

"Our oldest son introduced this recipe to our family years ago, and it is one of our favorites. I have shared it with so many friends, and every time I make it, of course I think of our son, Joshua, the pickiest eater in our family, and now the most gourmet of us all and a wonderful cook!"

Tricia Deitz, spouse of Sam Deitz, Dean of the College of Education

Serves 4

1 pint cherry tomatoes
½ cup sugar

Recipe Continues

⅓ cup sherry vinegar
2 garlic cloves, finely chopped
2 Tbsp. chopped fresh basil
1 scallion, thinly sliced
1 tsp. capers, drained
1 tsp. red pepper flakes

Tomatoes may be cut in half for a smoother marmalade. In a medium saucepan over medium heat, combine tomatoes and sugar; stir until sugar is dissolved. Add the vinegar, garlic, basil, scallion, capers, and red pepper flakes. Bring to a brisk simmer and cook for about 20 minutes, stirring frequently, until marmalade is syrupy and thick. Season with salt and pepper to taste and remove from heat. Pour into container and refrigerate for up to 5 days.

PER SERVING: Calories 116; Fat 0 g (Saturated 0 g); Cholesterol 0 mg; Sodium 27 mg; Carbohydrate 29.6 g; Fiber 1.4 g; Sugars 27.5 g; Protein 1.1 g

Rebecca's North Carolina Yellow Squash Casserole

"When my husband and I were in graduate school, our friend Rebecca often made this dish, from a recipe that came from her mother in North Carolina. Our own daughter Rebecca, now thirty-one, was named for our friend, and I always think of both of them when I make it."

Claudia Camp, John F. Weatherly Professor of Religion

Serves 8 to 10

2 lbs. yellow squash, cut into cubes
1 medium onion
1 tsp. salt

Recipe Continues

½ tsp. sugar
2 slightly beaten eggs
3 Tbsp. melted butter
3 Tbsp. flour
1 cup milk
½ lb. grated cheese
Enough bread crumbs mixed with some seasoned salt (or pre-seasoned bread crumbs) to cover the top of the casserole.

Bake at 325°. Put squash, onion, salt, and sugar in a pan with a small amount of water and simmer for about 20 minutes. Drain, then puree in blender on low speed. Stir in eggs and remaining ingredients except for bread crumbs. Bake in a 1½ to 2-qt. casserole approximately 60 minutes, or until done. (Note: cooking time will vary depending on the size and depth of the dish.) Spread the seasoned bread crumbs in a thick layer on top and cook 10 more minutes, or until center is firm.

PER SERVING: Calories 207; Fat 14.6 g (Saturated 9.1 g); Cholesterol 44 mg; Sodium 532 mg; Carbohydrate 9.5 g; Fiber 1.6 g; Sugars 4.4 g; Protein 10.8 g

Zucchini Vegetable Casserole

"This is the first recipe I requested after arriving at TCU and attending the first evening potluck supper sponsored by the TCU Faculty Women's Club (for couples) in the Reed Hall Faculty Center. It was a lovely room whose lighted glass cases cast a warm glow over the gathering. Many retirees have fond memories of the special times held in that special room."

Audie Vanderhoof, spouse of Bill Vanderhoof, Department of Education

Serves 8 to 10

4 zucchini
½ cup (1 stick) butter

Recipe Continues

1 small onion, chopped
1 cup corn kernels
1 (20-oz.) can tomatoes, drained
1 (4½-oz.) can chopped green chilies
2 cups grated Monterrey Jack cheese
Salt and pepper to taste

Bake at 350°. Slice zucchini into fourths lengthwise and then cut in chunks. Melt butter in skillet, then cook squash and onions about 15 or 20 minutes (until soft), stirring often. Add corn, chilies, tomatoes, salt, and pepper. Cook another 15 or 20 minutes, stirring occasionally. Add most of the cheese, leaving enough to sprinkle on top of the casserole. Put mixture into a casserole dish and sprinkle the top with remaining cheese. Heat in the oven until the cheese melts, about 5 to 10 minutes.

PER SERVING: Calories 289; Fat 23.9 g (Saturated 15.5 g); Cholesterol 64 mg; Sodium 405 mg; Carbohydrate 6.9 g; Fiber 1.6 g; Sugars 2.7 g; Protein 12.7 g

Gates at entrance to TCU campus. TCU Marketing and Communication.
Photo by Carolyn Cruz.

MAIN DISHES

Albuquerque Green Chile Stew

"This stew is delicious—and a cold-weather soporific agent."

Mary and David Metz, TCU Southwest Regional Director of Admissions

Serves 4

1 lb. very lean pork tenderloin, cubed
1 tsp. flour
3 large potatoes, diced
1 medium size onion, chopped
2 containers (8-oz. each) chopped green chilies (preferably Hatch), medium or hot
1 (14.5-oz.) can premium stewed tomatoes, thoroughly drained and rinsed
1 (15.5- or 16-oz.) can pinto beans, plain, drained and rinsed
1 (7-oz.) can Mexican-style corn, drained
1 (10-oz.) can Rotel Mexican-style diced tomatoes with lime juice and cilantro, drained
3 to 4 cups water
4 garlic cloves, mashed
salt to taste
oregano (optional; use only a tiny pinch)
2 tsp. dried cilantro

Toss the pork with the flour, then sauté (to help thicken the stew later). Sauté the potatoes and onions together. Put the pork, potatoes, and onions in a large pot. Add green chilies, drained stewed tomatoes, pinto beans, Mexican corn, and Rotel. Add water and mashed garlic. Salt to taste and add more water if necessary. Bring to a boil and simmer on low heat. If needed, add salt to taste. Garnish with 2 tsps. dried cilantro. Serve with warm flour tortillas.

PER SERVING: Calories 498; Fat 5.8 g (Saturated 1.6 g); Cholesterol 83 mg; Sodium 998 mg; Carbohydrate 72.1 g; Fiber 12.5 g; Sugars 10.5 g; Protein 40.4 g

Artichoke and Mushroom Lasagna

"This is our family's traditional Christmas Eve pasta."

Joan and Scott Sullivan, Dean, College of Fine Arts

Serves 8

Filling:
2 Tbsp. (¼ stick) butter
1 lb. mushrooms, sliced
3 garlic cloves, minced
2 (8-oz.) packages frozen artichoke hearts, thawed and coarsely chopped
½ cup dry vermouth

Béchamel sauce:
4½ Tbsp. butter
4½ Tbsp. all-purpose flour
4½ cups whole milk
2½ cups freshly grated Parmesan cheese (about 8 oz.)
ground nutmeg
1 (16-oz.) package oven-ready lasagna noodles
½ lb. whole milk mozzarella cheese, thinly sliced

Make filling: Melt butter in large skillet over medium high heat. Add mushrooms and garlic; sauté until mushrooms release juices and begin to brown, about 7 minutes. Add artichokes and vermouth. Cook until liquid is absorbed, stirring occasionally, about 10 minutes. Season with salt and pepper.

Make sauce: Melt butter in heavy medium saucepan over medium high heat. Add flour; stir 1 minute. Gradually whisk in milk. Reduce heat to medium and simmer until sauce thickens and lightly coats spoon, stirring occasionally, about 20 minutes. Stir in 1½ cups Parmesan cheese. Season to taste with salt, pepper, and ground nutmeg.

Recipe Continues

Bake at 350°. Spread ⅔ cup béchamel sauce over bottom of 9 x 13 x 2-in. glass baking dish. Top with enough noodles to cover bottom of dish. Spread ¼ of artichoke mixture over. Spoon ⅔ cup béchamel sauce over. Top béchamel with ¼ of mozzarella. Sprinkle with 3 Tbsp. Parmesan. Top with enough noodles to cover. Repeat layering 3 more times, finishing with a layer of noodles, then remaining béchamel. Sprinkle with remaining Parmesan. (Can be prepared 1 day ahead, covered with foil, and refrigerated.) Cover with foil and bake 1 hour, or 1 hour and 15 minutes if chilled. Remove foil. Increase temperature to 450°. Bake lasagna until golden on top, about 10 minutes longer.

PER SERVING: Calories 824; Fat 28.5 g (Saturated 16.2 g); Cholesterol 81 mg; Sodium 318 mg; Carbohydrate 100.1 g; Fiber 7.8 g; Sugars 11.1 g; Protein 40 g

Augie's Chili with Beans

"This was a recipe that my mother cooked and wrote out for me when I moved off campus and needed to cook for myself. As I was from Ohio and my mother was not used to or a fan of spicy food, it was a bit bland. So I added some hot spices to it and a can of beer for good measure."

Suzanne Huffman, Emeritus Professor, Schieffer College of Communication

Serves 6

1 lb. ground beef
1 chopped onion
1 Tbsp. chili powder
1 tsp. salt
dash garlic powder or 1 garlic clove, chopped
1 (1 lb. 4 oz.) can red kidney beans
1 (1 lb. 4 oz.) can crushed tomatoes

Recipe Continues

2 Tbsp. vinegar
½ to 1 tsp. sugar
1 (12-oz.) can beer
hot sauce to taste
red pepper to taste

Brown meat and, if necessary, remove excess fat. Add onions and cook until brown. Add remaining ingredients and simmer 45 minutes. Often better when reheated. Serve with saltine crackers or cornbread.

PER SERVING: Calories 266; Fat 7.5 g (Saturated 2.5 g); Cholesterol 68 mg; Sodium 670 mg; Carbohydrate 16.7 g; Fiber 5 g; Sugars 4.6 g; Protein 27.7 g

---

Belgian Beef Carbonnade

Karen Stone, Director, Brown-Lupton Gallery and spouse of Howard Stone, Professor of Pastoral Theology, Brite School of Divinity

Serves 8

3 to 4 lbs. beef for stew such as top blade steaks, short ribs, or chuck roast, trimmed and cut in 1-inch squares
3 Tbsp. cooking oil
2 to 3 lbs. yellow (not sweet) onions, halved crosswise, then sliced lengthwise about ¼ inch thick (about 8 cups)
1 Tbsp. tomato paste
1 to 3 garlic cloves, minced or pressed
3 Tbsp. flour
¾ cup low sodium chicken broth
¾ cup low sodium beef broth
12 oz. beer such as Newcastle brown ale, O'Doul's Amber N/A or Belgian-style ale
4 sprigs fresh thyme, tied together
2 bay leaves

Recipe Continues

1 Tbsp. cider vinegar
2 mashed anchovies
splash of soy sauce
salt and pepper to taste
1 to 2 packets gelatin, optional

Adjust oven rack to lower middle and preheat to 300°. Dry beef thoroughly and season with salt and pepper. Heat 2 Tbsp. oil in Dutch oven over medium high heat until beginning to smoke; add about one-third of beef and cook without moving until well browned on 2 sides, 2 to 4 minutes per side. Transfer beef to bowl and repeat with more oil and another third of the beef. If drippings in pot are very dark, add some of the chicken broth and deglaze. Repeat with final third of beef. Add remaining Tbsp. oil to empty pot and reduce to medium-low. Add onions, ½ tsp. salt, and tomato paste. Cook, scraping bottom of pot with wooden spoon, until onions have released some moisture, about 5 min. Increase heat to medium and continue to cook, stirring occasionally, until onions are lightly browned, 12 to 14 min. Stir in garlic and cook until fragrant, about 30 sec. Add flour and stir until onions are evenly coated and flour is lightly browned, about 2 min. Stir in chicken and beef broth, scraping pot bottom to loosen mixture. Stir in beer, thyme, bay leaves, vinegar, sugar, soy sauce, anchovy paste, browned beef with accumulated juices, and salt and pepper to taste. Sprinkle over a packet or two (depends on how thick you want it to get) of gelatin and stir in. Increase heat to medium high and bring to full simmer, stirring occasionally; cover partially, then put in oven. Cook until tender, about 2 hours. Discard thyme and bay leaves. Adjust seasonings with salt and pepper and serve.

PER SERVING: Calories 596; Fat 26 g (Saturated 8.2 g); Cholesterol 206 mg; Sodium 222 mg; Carbohydrate 15.7 g; Fiber 3 g; Sugars 5.5 g; Protein 68.4 g

Cajun Shrimp Boil

"Over the years I have ordered and eaten Cajun shrimp boil in various restaurants, mostly in South Texas, Louisiana, and Alabama. Many serve it on butcher paper, and it is an eat-with-your-hands family-style dish. Shrimp are typically not peeled. My most frequent complaint was that the shrimp were over-done and too soft. I knew how to solve this problem. I found 4 to 5 recipes for the dish in various places, spread them out, and picked and chose my ingredients. Most recipes are pretty similar in terms of ingredients. My contribution was having firm and tasty shrimp. You will notice from my recipe that I add shrimp nearly at the end of the process, boiling them for only two minutes before I remove the shrimp, sausage, and vegetables with a slotted spoon. The shrimp will be done and pink. I place the whole mixture on a large platter and serve family-style.

"A little extra tip is to only boil shrimp for three minutes. If you peel your shrimp before you cook them, clean over a bowl and add shells to the water. It will add to the flavor."

Chuck Lamb, Emeritus M.J. Neeley Professor of Marketing, Neeley School

Serves 8

2 lemons, halved
1 package shrimp or crab boil
8 small cloves garlic, diced
2 bay leaves
6 sprigs fresh thyme
salt and pepper to taste
8 small red potatoes, washed
1½ lbs. andouille sausage
4 ears corn, shucked
8 small boiler onions with skins removed
2 to 3 lb. large shrimp
3 Tbsp. butter

Recipe Continues

Fill a large pot with 4 quarts of water. Squeeze lemons into water and add lemon peels. Add shrimp or crab boil. Add bay leaves, garlic, and thyme. Add salt and pepper to taste. Cover and bring water to a boil, then reduce to a simmer. Add potatoes and sausage; simmer 5 minutes. Add corn and onions and simmer 5 more minutes. Add shrimp and bring water to a boil. Boil for 2 more minutes. Immediately remove shrimp, sausage, and all vegetables to a platter with a slotted spoon. Discard boiling bag if used. Melt butter in one cup of broth using low heat. Pour butter mix over shrimp and vegetables and serve.

PER SERVING: Calories 683; Fat 28.9 g (Saturated 11 g); Cholesterol 222 mg; Sodium 1228 mg; Carbohydrate 64.9 g; Fiber 7.9 g; Sugars 8.8 g; Protein 45.6 g

Chicken Pot Pie

"When we lived in Atlanta, I had a dear group of friends who met every Wednesday morning for breakfast at a restaurant, The American Roadhouse, in the Virginia-Highlands neighborhood. We put our favorite recipes into a cookbook, and I was so pleased to be able to include my chicken pot pie recipe. Another wonderful memory connected to this recipe is that it was published in the Star-Telegram *years ago in a story by Catherine Mallette about 'Comfort Foods,' and I was proud to have been included with my picture in the paper with my pot pie!"*

Tricia Deitz, spouse of Sam Deitz, Dean of the College of Education

Serves 6

1 broiler-fryer, cut up
1 tsp. salt
¼ tsp. pepper
1 lb. small yellow onions, quartered
1 lb. carrots, pared and cut in half lengthwise, then cut into 1-inch pieces
1 (10-oz.) package frozen peas

Recipe Continues

¼ cup (½ stick) butter or margarine
¼ cup all-purpose flour
¼ tsp. leaf thyme, crumbled
1 tsp. salt
¼ tsp. pepper
1 cup water
5 Tbsp. instant nonfat dry milk (or use 1 cup low-fat milk if you don't have dry milk)
Pie pastry

Bake at 400°. Place chicken in a large kettle or Dutch oven with enough water to cover. Bring to boiling and skim off foam. Add 1 tsp. salt and ¼ tsp. pepper. Lower heat; cover; simmer 30 minutes or until chicken is tender. Remove chicken from broth and let cool. Add onions and carrots to broth; bring to boiling; lower heat; simmer 10 minutes or until vegetables are just tender; add peas. Drain vegetables and reserve stock. Measure out 1 cup of stock. Meanwhile, skin and bone chicken. Cut into bite-size pieces. Combine with vegetables in a large bowl. Melt butter in a medium size saucepan. Add flour, thyme, and remaining salt and pepper; cook, stirring, 1 minute. Stir water into dry milk in a small bowl (skip this if you use low-fat milk); stir milk mixture into saucepan with the reserved 1 cup chicken stock. Cook, stirring constantly until thickened and bubbly. Pour over chicken and vegetables; stir to coat thoroughly. Spoon into a 2-quart deep round casserole. The pie pastry can be cut into strips and woven into a lattice over the top or be creative with your own design. Bake in oven for 30 minutes; pastry topping should be done and golden brown.

Note: You can use only chicken breasts for this, or a roasted chicken from the deli; you will have to make your own chicken broth with bouillon cubes to cook the vegetables; reserve a cup of the liquid for the sauce if you use an already-cooked chicken. This recipe can also be split between two smaller-sized casserole dishes.

PER SERVING: Calories 537; Fat 29.4 g (Saturated 10.3 g); Cholesterol 78 mg; Sodium 1219 mg; Carbohydrate 481 g; Fiber 5.7 g; Sugars 24.6 g; Protein 21.1 g

Chicken Tava (Turkish Chicken)

"For several years our son-in-law was stationed at the USAF base in Adana, Turkey. In order to visit our daughter and two young granddaughters, we 'had to' travel to Turkey. We had a wonderful time discovering this amazing country with equally amazing food. Chicken Tava was one of our favorites. My daughter created this recipe, with further modifications from me. It's best accompanied with real Turkish Pride bread, for which you can probably find a recipe online, but warmed-up pita from the grocery store is fine."

Karen Stone, Director, Brown-Lupton Gallery and spouse of Howard Stone, Professor of Pastoral Theology, Brite School of Divinity

Serves 4

1 lb. skinless, boneless chicken breasts, cut in medium-sized chunks
1 large yellow onion, coarsely chopped
2 Tbsp. olive oil (or less)
½ green pepper, coarsely chopped
2 (10-oz.) cans Hunt's fire-roasted diced tomatoes
4 to 6 garlic cloves, peeled
6 Tbsp. red pepper paste* (sweet or mild), mixed with 3 Tbsp. water
Salt and pepper to taste
Aleppo chili pepper* or your choice, to taste—more for spicier flavor
Crumbled feta, goat cheese, or other mild white cheese, to taste

Preheat oven to 400°. Season chicken pieces with salt and pepper. In a Dutch oven or heavy oven-proof pot, heat olive oil on medium heat until shimmering, then sauté onions for 4 to 5 minutes, stirring. When onions are translucent, add chicken pieces and brown quickly. Pour in tomatoes and red pepper paste and mix. Add more water and/or red pepper paste to taste. Add whole garlic cloves and chili pepper.

Cook on stove top and taste until desired flavor is reached, then place pot in oven and cook 20 to 30 minutes. In the last 10 minutes top with cheese. If desired, drizzle a small amount of olive oil on top of each serving. Serve with pilaf or plain brown rice.

Recipe Continues

*Sweet pepper paste and Aleppo chili pepper can be found at Trader Joe's.
PER SERVING: Calories 254; Fat 11.1 g (Saturated 2.5 g); Cholesterol 66 mg; Sodium 353 mg; Carbohydrate 11.8 g; Fiber 3.1 g; Sugars 3.8 g; Protein 26.6 g

Coq Au Vin

"My mother, Esther Winesanker, never liked cooking ordinary meals. To vary the repertoire, she collected many recipes that filled oversized catalog drawers in her kitchen. One such drawer contained hundreds of recipes for chicken dishes, many of which she tried out on us. A recipe that she returned to many times was 'Coq au vin,' which became a family favorite. Pressure-cooking fell out of favor after a while, but it is now in vogue again."

Miriam Levy, daughter of Michael Winesanker, Professor of Musicology and Chair of the Music Department, and Esther Winesanker, Library

Serves 4 to 6

2 Tbsp. vegetable oil
1 chicken, cut up
12 pearl onions, fresh or frozen
1 clove garlic, peeled and minced
1 tsp. salt
¼ tsp. thyme
1 small bay leaf
½ cup dry red wine
1 tsp. Kitchen Bouquet
1 (4-oz.) can of mushrooms, sliced and sautéed in butter (drain and reserve liquid for later)
parsley, to taste

Sauce:

Recipe Continues

2 Tbsp. flour
2 Tbsp. butter

Requires a pressure cooker.

Heat the oil in a skillet. Brown the chicken pieces and remove from pan. Lightly brown the onions and remove from pan. Pour the oil and scraped pieces adhering to bottom of skillet into pressure cooker. Add the garlic and chicken pieces. Sprinkle with salt and thyme, then add the bay leaf. Combine the wine and Kitchen Bouquet and pour over the chicken. Cook at full pressure 10 minutes. Allow pressure cooker to cool. Cut the carrot into strips about ¾ x 2 inches. Add the carrots, onions, and mushrooms, including liquid from mushrooms. Cook at full pressure 4 minutes. Cool at once and remove chicken and vegetables to serving platter. Make the sauce by stirring the flour and butter into the pan juices and cook uncovered, stirring until thick; pour over chicken and vegetables and garnish with parsley.

PER SERVING: Calories 489; Fat 17.6 g (Saturated 4.2 g); Cholesterol 125 mg; Sodium 718 mg; Carbohydrate 32.7 g; Fiber 7.3 g; Sugars 14.7 g; Protein 45 g

Doris's Casserole

"This is a family favorite, beloved by all but one of my children (she doesn't like cream cheese, sour cream, etc.). It was served to me at a dinner party nearly fifty years go by a woman named Doris. I didn't see much of Doris in later years, but when I did she barely remembered the casserole. I gave the recipe to a friend who insisted the noodle layer should come first. I assured her it shouldn't. This is supposed to feed six, but it disappears quickly."

Judy Alter, Director, TCU Press

Serves 6

Recipe Continues

First layer:
1 lb. ground beef
1 (14-oz.) can diced tomatoes
1 (8-oz.) can tomato sauce
2 cloves garlic, crushed in garlic press
2 tsp. each sugar and salt (I cut back on those, but sugar is important in tomato-based sauces—my mom taught me years ago it sort of rounds it off.)
Pepper to taste

Brown ground beef in skillet. Drain grease and return to skillet. Add tomatoes and tomato sauce, garlic, sugar, salt, and pepper. Simmer 20 minutes, until it thickens a little. Spread in a 9 x 13-in. pan.

Second (noodle) layer:
1 (5-oz.) (approximately—they don't come in this size pkg.) egg noodles
1 (3-oz.) package cream cheese (here again, you have to fudge; cream cheese doesn't come in a 3-oz. package anymore)
1 cup sour cream
6 green onions chopped, with some of the tops included

Topping:
1½ cups grated cheddar cheese

Bake at 350°. Cook egg noodles and drain. While the noodles are hot, stir in cream cheese, sour cream, and green onions. Spread over meat mixture. Top with grated cheddar, and bake 35 minutes or until bubbly and cheese is slightly browned.

PER SERVING: Calories 451; Fat 27.8 g (Saturated 16 g); Cholesterol 137 mg; Sodium 1268 mg; Carbohydrate 15.7 g; Fiber 2.1 g; Sugars 5.4 g; Protein 34.7 g

Elegant Chicken Crepes

"I was given this recipe by Mrs. Patsy Singleton who was a professor in TCU's School of Education for many years. She bequeathed her vast collection of recipes to me, and I found this one among them. It had written at the side, 'Served by W. at luncheon for Mildred.' When preparing this, I sometimes make the crepes, but buying them greatly simplifies the prep. The dish can be made ahead and kept in the refrigerator until time to cook."

Mary Jo Clegg, spouse of Luther Clegg, Emeritus Professor of Education

Serves 12

Cream sauce:
6 Tbsp. butter
6 Tbsp. flour
½ tsp. salt
2 cups chicken broth
1 cup heavy cream
½ tsp. black pepper
¼ tsp. nutmeg

Crepe filling:
6 Tbsp. butter, melted
½ cup onions, finely chopped
¼ cup celery, finely chopped
½ lb. mushrooms, sliced
2 cups cooked chicken, diced
½ cup toasted almonds, coarsely chopped
½ of cream sauce mixture
12 prepared, packaged crepes

First, prepare cream sauce:
Melt butter in saucepan until bubbly and whisk in flour and salt. Cook until smooth, stirring constantly (about 2 min.). Gradually add chicken broth, stirring constantly, and cook (stirring) until mixture begins to

Recipe Continues

thicken. Stir in cream, pepper, and nutmeg. Continue to stir and cook until smooth and slightly thick—2 or 3 minutes.

Prepare crepe filling:
Sauté onions and celery in melted butter until onions are translucent. Add mushrooms and cook for 3 to 4 min. Add chicken and almonds and cook, stirring, until chicken is heated. Add ½ of cream sauce and mix well.

Assemble the crepes:
Bake at 400°. Lay each crepe flat and fill with 3 Tbsp. filling, spreading down center of crepe. Fold sides toward the center and place in buttered pan. Fill and fold remaining crepes, placing them side by side in pan, then cover with remaining cream sauce and sprinkle with Parmesan cheese, if desired. Bake until hot and bubbly and top is lightly brown—about 20 minutes.

Per Serving: Calories 267; Fat 19.2 g (Saturated 10 g); Cholesterol 68 mg; Sodium 398 mg; Carbohydrate 13.4 g; Fiber 0.9 g; Sugars 4.9 g; Protein 10.8 g

Fantastic Fresh Tomato Sauce Pasta

"We often have a garden and especially enjoy the taste of fresh-from-the-garden tomatoes."

Suzanne Huffman, Emeritus Professor, Schieffer College of Communication

Serves 6

5 large, ripe tomatoes, chopped
½ cup olive oil
2 cloves garlic, sliced in half lengthwise
½ cup chopped fresh basil leaves

Recipe Continues

1 teaspoon salt
½ teaspoon red pepper flakes
1 lb. pasta, cooked and drained (linguine, spaghetti, angel hair, etc.)

Use tomatoes that are bursting with garden ripeness. Mix tomatoes, oil, garlic, basil, salt, and red pepper flakes in a large bowl. Let sit for about two hours. When ready to serve, remove garlic halves and toss tomato mixture with hot pasta.

PER SERVING: Calories 391; Fat 18.9 g (Saturated 2.7 g); Cholesterol 55 mg; Sodium 415 mg; Carbohydrate 47.7 g; Fiber 1.9 g; Sugars 10.5 g; Protein 10 g

Green Chile Chicken Stew

"I was introduced to Hatch chiles when we moved to Texas and just fell in love with these peppers. We have even ventured to Hatch, New Mexico, to see where they are grown. Now I make sure I buy lots of them when they are in season and freeze them to use throughout the year. This recipe has evolved over the years, and it has become a favorite with family and friends."

Cecilia Silva, Professor of Education

Serves 4 to 6

1 tsp. olive oil
3 cloves garlic, minced
1 onion, diced small
1 rotisserie chicken (skinned, deboned, and cut in small pieces)
1 tsp. ground cumin
1 tsp. dried thyme
1 tsp. dried basil leaf

Recipe Continues

3 to 6 Hatch chiles, seeded and chopped*
6 cups chicken broth
5 carrots, thinly sliced
5 stalks celery, chopped
½ cup corn
3 medium red potatoes, peeled and diced

Heat olive oil, add garlic and onion. Sauté until translucent. Add remaining ingredients. Simmer over medium heat until vegetables are tender (approximately 25 minutes). Season with salt and pepper to taste.

*I buy roasted Hatch chiles when they come out at the end of the summer and freeze them in small batches (3 to 4 per baggie).

PER SERVING: Calories 325; Fat 3.6 g (Saturated 0.6 g); Cholesterol 105 mg; Sodium 1340 mg; Carbohydrate 31.2 g; Fiber 4.2 g; Sugars 5.7 g; Protein 43.2 g

Ham Loaf with Raisin Sauce

"This recipe from my maternal grandmother has been served at Thanksgiving, Christmas, or Easter for many years and connects me to my maternal roots. The loaf offers a nice alternative to the usual turkey or ham at those holidays and is very heart healthy. My husband and I have found our local neighbors relish this loaf and sauce, an entrée they have never experienced. The loaf and sauce heat up well as leftovers and go nicely with a green salad and sweet potato dish."

Carolyn Spence Cagle, Emeritus Professor of Nursing

Serves 6 to 8

1 lb. ground smoked ham
1 lb. ground pork shoulder

Recipe Continues

1 cup crushed plain shredded wheat biscuits (about 2 large biscuits)
2 eggs
½ tsp. salt
Pepper, as desired
1 tsp. parsley
½ tsp. onion
1 Tbsp. brown sugar
1 scant Tbsp. dry mustard

Bake at 350°. Mix all ingredients and bake in a loaf pan for 1 hour; use a pan with a rack covered in aluminum foil to catch drippings.

Sauce:
1 Tbsp. flour
¼ tsp. dry mustard
2 cups raisins
1 cup sugar
1½ cups water
¼ cup vinegar

Cook ingredients in a saucepan over low to moderate heat until thick; add as desired to top off ham loaf servings.

PER SERVING: Calories 737; Fat 26 g (Saturated 9.5 g); Cholesterol 204 mg; Sodium 1142 mg; Carbohydrate 80.6 g; Fiber 2.8 g; Sugars 64.4 g; Protein 50 g

Hot Chicken Salad

"I introduced this recipe to my relatives after I had enjoyed it at a ladies' gathering. It never failed to get rave reviews at potlucks."

Cynthia Chapa, Department of Modern Language Studies, Instructor II of German

Recipe Continues

Serves 10

2 cups chopped cooked chicken
2 cups cooked rice
1 (10¾-oz.) can cream of chicken soup
3 hard-boiled eggs, chopped
1 cup diced celery
½ cup pimento, chopped
1½ tsp. pepper
¼ tsp. salt
½ cup slivered almonds
½ cup mayonnaise

Bake at 350°. Mix all ingredients together. Top with buttered bread crumbs and bake for 45 minutes. May be mixed together a day ahead.

PER SERVING: Calories 300; Fat 10.5 g (Saturated 2 g); Cholesterol 76 mg; Sodium 388 mg; Carbohydrate 36.4 g; Fiber 1.3 g; Sugars 1.7 g; Protein 14.4 g

Humble Hamburger with Baked Beans

"We found this recipe in the Chicago Tribune *(about 45 years ago!) when my mom and dad were visiting for Thanksgiving. Of course, everyone enjoys the turkey dinner and then all the wonderful leftovers, but this is an easy, different dish to feed a crowd some other time during the holiday or any time you're in the mood for something humble."*

Judy Groulx, Emeritus Associate Professor, College of Education

Serves 8

4 slices bacon, cut into 1-inch pieces
1 medium onion, chopped

Recipe Continues

1 lb. ground beef
1 tsp. salt
2 (16-oz.) cans pork and beans (undrained)
½ cup molasses
½ cup ketchup
2 tsp. Worcestershire
½ tsp. dry mustard

Bake at 375°. Grease a 2-qt. casserole dish. Cook bacon until crisp in a medium-to-large skillet, then drain it on paper towels and set aside. In the skillet, add onion and ground beef; sauté until meat is browned. Use a slotted spoon to remove to the casserole dish; then add salt and the bacon. After discarding the drippings, use skillet to heat the rest of the ingredients together. Pour into casserole with the meat and stir. Bake uncovered for 1 hour. Goes well with warm bread and a green salad or fruit salad.

PER SERVING: Calories 308; Fat 8.4 g (Saturated 2.9 g); Cholesterol 64 mg; Sodium 666 mg; Carbohydrate 33.3 g; Fiber 3.9 g; Sugars 19.6 g; Protein 24.2 g

Judy's Sloppy Joe

"A friend gave me a recipe for a wine casserole, which turned out so much like Sloppy Joes that I called it that when I served it. Recently my oldest daughter asked for the recipe and cooked it for her husband, who pronounced that it was really good, but it wasn't Sloppy Joes, which to him was meat and ketchup. (I think that's a simplistic description.) But she emailed me caustically that she guessed she was the only one who grew up thinking red wine was an essential ingredient of Sloppy Joes."

Judy Alter, Director, TCU Press

Recipe Continues

Serves 4 to 6

1 lb. ground beef
1 (15-oz.) can of beans (any kind you want), rinsed and drained
½ cup chopped onion
½ cup diced celery
2 Tbsp. bacon drippings (If you can bring yourself to use it in this health-conscious age, or use vegetable oil, but the bacon flavor really makes a difference.)
1½ cup ketchup
1½ Tbsp. Worcestershire
dash of Tabasco
1 tsp. salt
⅛ tsp. pepper
¼ tsp. oregano
¼ cup dry red wine
1 Tbsp. A-1 sauce (If I don't have this, I omit it; I can never tell the difference.)

Cook onion in bacon drippings. Add beef and brown. Add remaining ingredients and simmer 20 to 30 minutes. You can serve this on toasted buns or just in a bowl, like a stew.

PER SERVING: Calories 448; Fat 6.7 g (Saturated 2.3 g); Cholesterol 71 mg; Sodium 2755 mg; Carbohydrate 68.3 g; Fiber 5.2 g; Sugars 53.9 g; Protein 31.4 g

Korean Bar-Be-Que

"My mother, Josey Clark, was Korean, and this is what my family and I grew up eating. Everyone that has tried this recipe has loved it and it has now become their favorite."

Joe Ann May, Financial Assistant, Financial Services Department

Recipe Continues

Serves 4

1 lb. beef, not too lean
2 Tbsp. Kikkoman soy sauce
1 Tbsp. sugar
1 Tbsp. sesame oil
1 Tbsp. sesame salt
⅛ tsp. black pepper
4 medium green onions coarsely chopped
3 cloves garlic, finely chopped
1 tsp. fresh ginger, finely chopped
2 Tbsp. water, rice wine, or white wine
2 tsp. sesame seeds
Dash of Accent (optional)

Cut the beef into very thin slices (⅛-inch thick) or get butcher to do it. Marinate the beef in the ingredients for 1½ to 2 hours. Grill or pan fry.

Optional meats—beef short ribs (marinated overnight) or pork

Must try this special sauce:
½ cup Kikkoman soy sauce
1 tsp. sesame oil
1 tsp. red pepper (adjust to preferred heat)
1 tsp. sesame seed
½ tsp. garlic powder or minced garlic
2 to 3 green onions, finely chopped

Combine all ingredients and sprinkle over white rice.

PER SERVING: Calories 702; Fat 25.4 g (Saturated 8.6 g); Cholesterol 304 mg; Sodium 679 mg; Carbohydrate 6.3 g; Fiber 0.7 g; Sugars 3.6 g; Protein 10.5 g

Lasagna Mexicana

"This is one of my favorite quick-and-easy dinner meals. My mother-in-law gave me this recipe years ago."

Linda Smith, Director, Graduate Program Admissions, Neeley School

Serves 6

1 lb. hamburger
½ cup chopped onion
¼ cup taco seasoning
1 (8-oz.) can of tomato sauce or salsa
1 (16-oz.) can Mexi-Beans (w/chili gravy)
1 (15-oz.) can black beans
1 (4-oz.) can green chilies
6 tortillas (any variety)
2 cups shredded cheese of choice

Bake at 350°. Brown hamburger and onion. Drain. Stir in taco seasoning, tomato sauce, beans, and chilies. Layer half of tortillas on bottom of a 12 x 8-in. baking dish. Spread half of the meat mixture over the tortillas and sprinkle with half of the shredded cheese. Repeat layers. Bake for 30 minutes. Let stand 10 minutes before serving. Serve with a salad for a complete meal.

PER SERVING: Calories 461; Fat 19.1 g (Saturated 10.3 g); Cholesterol 97 mg; Sodium 1184 mg; Carbohydrate 33.2 g; Fiber 8.2 g; Sugars 3 g; Protein 37.7 g

Mom's Company Stew

"This was my mother's 'company stew.' I suspect she got it out of the Kansas City Star, *but really have no idea. She didn't make up recipes, so it came intact from somewhere. It's a great dish to stick in the oven in the morning to serve for dinner. The whole house smells so tempting and good. Mom and I usually serve it over brown rice with a fresh green salad, French baguette, and a nice red wine. It's not your usual stew! Some of the keys to this recipe's success are NOT opening the pot or stirring it, using WHITE wine in the mixture, and using good meat. I used to buy a chuck roast and cut it up, but now I buy beef stew meat from Central Market and cut it into smaller pieces.*

Jean Walbridge, Assistant to the Chancellor, Secretary to Board of Trustees

Serves 6 to 8

2 lbs. beef stew meat, cut into bite-size pieces
3 large carrots, cleaned and cut into chunks
3 small onions, peeled and cut into chunks
½ (10.5-oz.) can beef consommé
1 (15-oz. or larger) can petite cut tomatoes
1 (15-oz. or larger) can peas, or frozen peas
½ cup white wine
4 Tbsp. minute tapioca
1 Tbsp. brown sugar
½ cup plain breadcrumbs
1 bay leaf
salt and pepper

Combine and stir all ingredients in a Dutch oven. Cover. Cook at 250° for six or seven hours. DO NOT PEEK OR STIR.

PER SERVING: Calories 345; Fat 7.7 g (Saturated 2.8 g); Cholesterol 101 mg; Sodium 187 mg; Carbohydrate 25.6 g; Fiber 5 g; Sugars 8 g; Protein 39.2 g

Oven-Baked Salmon

"Of course, there are many recipes for cooking salmon; that's good since it means that we'll never grow tired of this healthy entrée. However, I've found this recipe, along with a glass of white wine, makes for easy preparation and an enjoyable meal. It's a weekly favorite at the Adams's house!"

Larry D. Adams, Associate Provost for Academic Affairs and Associate Professor of Sociology

Serves 2

1 (6 to 8 oz.) salmon fillet
salt and pepper
1 tsp. lemon juice
2 Tbsp. honey mustard
3 Tbsp. honey

Bake at 375°. Salt and pepper salmon to taste. In a small bowl, stir together lemon juice, honey mustard, and honey (it's okay to adjust ingredients of the mixture to taste). Marinate salmon in mixture for 15 to 20 minutes; drain. Place salmon in an aluminum foil-lined baking dish and bake, uncovered, for 18 to 20 minutes, or until salmon flakes easily with a fork. Serve warm, or salmon may be served cold; e.g., over a bed of salad.

Suggestion: Serve with roasted asparagus, tossed salad, or other green vegetable.

PER SERVING: Calories 277; Fat 7 g (Saturated 1 g); Cholesterol 50 mg; Sodium 127 mg; Carbohydrate 32 g; Fiber 0.1 g; Sugars 28.9 g; Protein 22.1 g

Pork and Apples

"This dish is especially good on a winter's day, or before a football game against Arkansas. My mother used to prepare sliced, unpeeled Jonathan apples combined with sliced onion sautéed in butter when she served fried pork chops, which was the taste combination that inspired this dish."

Judith Oelfke Smith, Associate Director of University Publications
Emmet G. Smith, Emeritus Herndon Professor of Organ and Church Music

Serves 4 to 6

2 one-inch (10-oz.) thick pork loin chops
2 cups coarsely chopped onion
1 (15-oz.) can chicken broth (I use low-sodium Swanson's)
2 Tbsp. fresh lemon juice
½ tsp. salt
Original "Mrs. Dash" or freshly ground black pepper to taste
Three or four large apples (I prefer Pink Lady), peeled, cored, and sliced ¼-inch thick
1 to 2 Tbsp. maple syrup to taste, depending on sweetness of apples
1 Tbsp. butter

Pat the chops dry, and slice each cross-ways into five or six ½-inch strips. Trim off most of the fat and render it in a large, heavy Dutch oven over medium high heat, coating the bottom of the pot; discard the remains.

On a large plate, coat the sliced meat with oil and sprinkle with salt. Brown the meat in the Dutch oven in two batches.

Return all the meat to the Dutch oven and add the sliced onion. Add the 15-oz. can chicken broth, lemon juice, and seasonings. Cover and simmer for 1½ hours over a medium-low heat until the meat is very tender.

Before adding the apples, I like to break the slices of meat into chunks with a wooden spoon. Add the sliced apples and 1 Tbsp. butter. Simmer covered for another 30 to 40 minutes until the apples are tender and

Recipe Continues

transparent. Add the maple syrup to taste and adjust seasoning. Serve in shallow soup bowls. A green salad goes well with this dish.

PER SERVING: Calories 379; Fat 11.7 g (Saturated 4.4 g); Cholesterol 135 mg; Sodium 475 mg; Carbohydrate 72.1 g; Fiber 3.5 g; Sugars 15.5 g; Protein 46 g

Pork en Croute

"This recipe comes from my older sister. It is so well-liked that everyone in her family tries to claim credit for originating the dish."

Donna Johnson, Executive Assistant to the Provost

Serves 6 to 8

1 frozen (17.3-oz.) package Pepperidge Farm Pastry Sheets, thawed
1 bunch of scallions, cleaned and chopped
Dijon mustard
1 pork tenderloin (1 pound)

Bake at 350°. Roll out the pastry and place the pork tenderloin in the middle. Cut the tenderloin along its length, not cutting all the way through. Line the opening with mustard and fill evenly with the chopped scallions. Seal the tenderloin in the pastry like an egg roll and bake for 25 to 35 minutes. Remove from oven and let rest before slicing.

While pork is baking prepare the bordelaise sauce:
1 (1.2-oz.) envelope Knorr Demi-Glace or Classic Brown Sauce, prepared as directed on package
2 Tbsp. cranberry or raspberry preserves or jelly
Red wine to taste

Recipe Continues

Combine ingredients and heat. Serve over the pork.

PER SERVING: Calories 324; Fat 17.1 g (Saturated 8.2 g); Cholesterol 41 mg; Sodium 265 mg; Carbohydrate 24 g; Fiber 1.7 g; Sugars 1.7 g; Protein 19.5 g

Shrimp Casserole

"This recipe was given to me by my boss in the mid-1960s. She said it would win your boyfriend's heart. Look what happened—I married Scott!"

Joan Sullivan, spouse of Scott Sullivan, Dean of Fine Arts

Serves 6 to 8

1 lb. raw shrimp (medium or large), unpeeled
1 Tbsp. lemon juice
3 Tbsp. salad oil
1 cup regular rice, uncooked
2 Tbsp. butter
¼ cup minced green pepper
¼ cup minced onion
1 tsp. salt
⅛ tsp. pepper
⅛ tsp. mace
Dash cayenne pepper
1 (10.5-oz.) can tomato soup
1 cup heavy cream
½ cup sherry
¾ cup slivered almonds

Bake at 350°. Cook shrimp in boiling, salted water to cover for 3 to 5 minutes. Drain. Peel and devein. Place in 2-quart casserole dish; sprinkle with lemon juice and oil, then chill. Meanwhile, cook rice as package label directs. In butter, sauté green pepper and onion until tender. Add

Recipe Continues

vegetables to rice, along with salt, pepper, spices, soup, cream, sherry, and ½ cup almonds; toss well. Reserve 8 of the shrimp for topping, then spread the rice mixture over the remaining shrimp and bake uncovered 35 minutes. Top with the reserved shrimp and the rest of the almonds. Bake 20 minutes longer.

PER SERVING: Calories 508; Fat 26 g (Saturated 8.6 g); Cholesterol 197 mg; Sodium 889 mg; Carbohydrate 36.7 g; Fiber 2.7 g; Sugars 5 g; Protein 23.3 g

South Texas Seafood Gumbo

"The inspiration for this dish came from the Corpus Christi Junior League Cookbook. I combined what I liked from three or four recipes and have modified them to my taste over the years. Two keys to making good gumbo are making a dark, homemade roux and not overcooking the seafood. "

Chuck Lamb, Emeritus M.J. Neeley Professor of Marketing, Neeley School

Serves 6

Roux:
5 Tbsp. bacon grease or lard
5 Tbsp. flour

Fold flour into fat and stir on low heat for about 30 minutes, or until mixture turns dark brown to black. Avoid burning roux but heat close to that point.

Gumbo:
2 large onions, chopped
2 bell peppers, chopped
3 stalks of celery, chopped
6 to 8 garlic cloves, chopped

Recipe Continues

32 oz. chicken stock
2 (15-oz.) cans of chopped tomatoes
1 (10-oz.) can of original Rotel tomatoes
1 (15-oz.) can of tomato sauce
1 to 2 links of Kielbasa sausage, halved lengthwise and sliced
1 lb. of sliced fresh okra, or 2 (14.5 oz.) cans of Trappey's gumbo okra with juice
1 tsp. salt
1 tsp. pepper
4 sprigs of fresh parsley, chopped
2 bay leaves
½ tsp. thyme
½ tsp. cayenne pepper
1 tsp. Worchester sauce
½ tsp. Tabasco sauce
Raw redfish or black drum fish (or other fresh fin fish), cubed
5 to 6 lbs. of raw, peeled shrimp
Filé spice (optional)
Cooked rice
Additional, optional ingredients: oysters, fish, chicken, crab meat, crawfish

To make gumbo add onions, peppers, celery, garlic, and small amount of the chicken stock to roux. Sauté until vegetables soften. Add the remainder of the chicken stock, the canned tomatoes, Rotel tomatoes, tomato sauce, sausage, okra, salt, pepper, spices, and Worchester and Tabasco sauces. Bring mix to a boil and simmer as long as you like—at least 1 hour. When ready to serve, place a small amount of gumbo in a smaller pot. Bring to a boil. Add cubed redfish or whatever fish you are using. Boil for about 3 minutes. Add peeled shrimp. Boil for three more minutes only—longer will make shrimp tough. Add filé, if using. Return fish and gumbo mix to large pot.

For each serving, place gumbo over a scoop of rice (or vice versa, as desired) in a soup bowl. Sprinkle with fresh parsley.

Gumbo can be frozen.

Recipe Continues

PER SERVING: Calories 766; Fat 30 g (Saturated 11.4 g); Cholesterol 743 mg; Sodium 2931 mg; Carbohydrate 39.5 g; Fiber 5.2 g; Sugars 15.3 g; Protein 87.2 g

Stuffed Pasta Shells

Kathryn Schruba, Coordinator of Admission Office Services

Serves 4 to 6

Ingredients for filling:
2 cups ricotta cheese
Pepper to taste
¾ cup mozzarella cheese, shredded
1 Tbsp. parsley (preferably fresh)
2 eggs, slightly beaten
¼ cup Romano cheese, finely grated
1 tsp. salt

Combine filling ingredients in a large bowl and mix thoroughly. Set aside.

Pasta:
1 recipe spaghetti sauce, or one jar prepared spaghetti sauce
1 lb. large shell pasta, cooked as directed on package

Bake at 350°. Spread part of the sauce on bottom of large 9 x 13-in. lasagna pan. Stuff shells with filling and place in rows in lasagna pan. Cover with remaining sauce. Sprinkle with additional Romano or shredded mozzarella cheese. Cover pan with aluminum foil. Bake for 30 to 45 minutes.

PER SERVING: Calories 557; Fat 22 g (Saturated 12.3 g); Cholesterol 1788 mg; Sodium 1567 mg; Carbohydrate 52.9 g; Fiber 1.5 g; Sugars 4.9 g; Protein 37.4 g

Sweet and Sour Chicken

"My mother, Esther Winesanker, enjoyed entertaining, and, as the Music Department Chair's wife, had many opportunities to do so. Depending on the number of people she was hosting, she might make one, two, or even three of these recipes. Our family always hoped that there would be leftovers, because we loved this dish."

Miriam Levy, daughter of Michael Winesanker, Professor of Musicology and Chair of the Music Department, and Esther Winesanker, Library

Serves 10 to 12

4½ lbs. chicken breasts
1½ Tbsp. vegetable oil
1 medium onion, chopped
⅜ cup green pepper, diced
2 cloves garlic, chopped fine, then mashed
⅜ cup brown sugar
5 Tbsp. flour
1½ cups water
¼ tsp. ginger powder
¼ tsp. dry mustard
¾ tsp. salt
3 Tbsp. soy sauce
juice of one lemon
1 cup Heinz chili sauce (perhaps a bit more)
10 to 12 pineapple rings
⅜ cup pineapple juice
1½ apples, unpeeled and sliced thin
1½ cans water chestnuts, sliced, plus liquid
1 (14-oz.) can bean sprouts, plus some liquid
2 Tbsp. Chinese brown gravy

Bake at 350°. Cut chicken breasts into cubes and bake for 20 to 30 minutes, or until no longer pink. In a large skillet, heat 1½ Tbsp. vegetable oil and add the onion, green pepper, garlic, and brown sugar. Make a paste with the 5 Tbsp. of flour and ½ cup of water. Add the paste to the

Recipe Continues

onion and green pepper mixture, then gradually stir in 1 cup of water. To this mixture, add the ginger, dry mustard, salt, soy sauce, lemon juice, chili sauce, pineapple and juice, apples, water chestnuts, bean sprouts, and brown gravy. Cook for 30 minutes, stirring occasionally. If too much liquid, add more thickening. Add chicken pieces and bake for about 30 minutes.

PER SERVING: Calories 533; Fat 17.8 g (Saturated 4.6 g); Cholesterol 182 mg; Sodium 1274 mg; Carbohydrate 29.3 g; Fiber 2.6 g; Sugars 18.9 g; Protein 62.9 g

Venison Scaloppini with Chipotle Cream Sauce

"I created this recipe one Christmas Eve when Howard and I were staying in a romantic little adobe in a remote part of New Mexico. It was 10 miles to a tiny town with a general store that had a limited range of goods, so we had to be creative!"

Karen Stone, Director, Brown-Lupton Gallery and spouse of Howard Stone, Professor of Pastoral Theology, Brite School of Divinity

Serves 2

3 backstrap (tenderloin) steaks of venison
½ cup flour
pepper, freshly cracked
salt (optional)
¾ Tbsp. of olive oil/grapeseed oil/butter mixture
6 oz. good, dry sherry (do not use cooking sherry—or if you are far from civilization and that's all you can get, add no other salt to the recipe)
½ cup homemade chicken stock (unsalted), or Better than Bouillon mixed a bit weaker than directed on the jar
1 cup dried, soaked (reconstituted) shiitake mushrooms or fresh mush-

Recipe Continues

rooms (experiment with different varieties)
approximately ¼ cup mushroom liquor from soaking
approximately ⅓ cup chipotle sauce (or to taste). You can seed and finely chop 1 or 2 canned chipotles in adobo sauce plus a teaspoon or more (to taste) of the adobo sauce
5 oz. evaporated whole milk or half and half

Place ovenproof dish in oven and heat to 250.° Cut venison tenderloin (backstrap) steaks in half, then cut horizontally and butterfly (resulting in six butterflied, very thin scaloppini). If you do not have tenderloin, cut meat into small pieces, place between sheets of plastic wrap, and pound to approximately ⅛-in. thickness. Mix together the flour, pepper, and salt (no salt if using cooking sherry). Dredge the venison in the flour mixture. Heat butter/olive oil/grapeseed oil mixture in a heavy-bottom frying pan until a drop of water dances and sizzles. Sauté the venison on medium high for about one minute or less per side. Place the sautéed meat in the heated baking dish and return the dish to the oven.

Pour half of the sherry in the pan used for sautéing the meat. Add the chicken broth, the chipotle sauce, and the evaporated milk or half and half. Squeeze the liquid out of the mushrooms with hands and put on the plate with flour left over from the venison, stir around to coat, and add to the pan with the sherry mixture, stirring to prevent lumps. Add a little of the mushroom liquid and the rest of the sherry to the pan; adjust chipotle to taste; add more sherry or stock if needed; simmer and stir until sauce is slightly thickened and smooth. When sauce is the desired consistency and flavor, turn heat down and keep warm. Remove venison from oven. Place each scaloppini of venison in the sauce, then put on serving plate and top with more sauce; repeat (three pieces per plate, or two if there are several other dishes being served).

Variation: Use Marsala wine instead of sherry; omit chipotle.

PER SERVING: Calories 586; Fat 10.3 g (Saturated 3 g); Cholesterol 71 mg; Sodium 600 mg; Carbohydrate 46.8 g; Fiber 2.4 g; Sugars 14.6 g; Protein 32.3 g

White Bean Chili with Chicken

"I received this recipe from a high school friend who served it at a high school get-together."

Joan Yates, Administrative Assistant, International Admissions

Serves 6 to 8

1 lb. white (northern) beans, soaked overnight
7 cups chicken broth
2 cloves garlic, minced
1 tsp. pepper
1 tsp. salt
1 Tbsp. oregano
1 Tbsp. cumin
1 (4.5-oz.) can green chilies
5 cups cooked chicken, such as rotisserie chicken
8 flour tortillas (optional: I prefer to serve chili with small cornbread muffins on the side instead of using tortillas)

Drain and rinse beans. Simmer first 8 ingredients 1½ to 2 hours. Add chicken and chilies and simmer another ½ hour. If using tortillas, line bowls with tortillas and cover with chili. This chili is delicious without extras, but you can add any combination of shredded jack cheese, black olives, salsa, sour cream, and/or avocado, if you wish. Double recipe for larger group.

PER SERVING: Calories 285; Fat 4.8 g (Saturated 1.3 g); Cholesterol 67 mg; Sodium 761 mg; Carbohydrate 23.6 g; Fiber 5.4 g; Sugars 1 g; Protein 35.6 g

Robert Carr Chapel at TCU. TCU Marketing and Communication.
Photo by Amy Peterson.

DESSERTS

Apple Cake

Nancy Grieser, Director of Brite Housing

Serves 12

Bake at 350°

¾ cup butter
1 cup sugar
2 eggs
2 cups flour
2 tsp. baking powder
¾ tsp. salt
1½ tsp. cinnamon
1 tsp. vanilla
1 (20-oz.) can low-sugar apple pie filling

Streusel:
⅓ cup butter
⅓ cup sugar
⅔ cup flour
1 tsp. cinnamon

Cream butter and sugar; beat in 2 eggs and set aside. Mix together flour, baking powder, salt, and cinnamon. Add to creamed mixture and add vanilla. Spread all but ¾ cup batter in buttered and floured 9 x 13-in. baking dish. Spread 1 can low-sugar apple pie filling over batter. Drop reserved batter by tablespoons on apple filling and swirl with table knife. Mix together streusel ingredients. Top batter with streusel and bake 45 minutes or until inserted toothpick comes out clean.

To make Cherry Streusel Cake: Eliminate cinnamon from ingredients for batter and streusel. Add a teaspoon almond extract and substitute a can of cherry pie filling for apple pie filling.

Recipe Continues

PER SERVING: Calories 352; Fat 17.6 g (Saturated 10.8 g); Cholesterol 71 mg; Sodium 279 mg; Carbohydrate 46.1 g; Fiber 0.9 g; Sugars 23.5 g; Protein 4 g

Apple Dumplings

"When my husband first came to TCU, the School of Ed faculty and staff shared a common room they used as a workroom, coffee bar, and a place to visit. At Christmas time, 'goodies' were brought to this room to share. Many delicious recipes came from those happy times. This recipe came from Lois Patterson, wife of Dr. Henry Patterson, Professor of Special Education, who was an excellent cook. Both Lois and Henry were enthusiastic supporters of Women's Basketball at TCU. They are sorely missed."

Mary Jo Clegg, spouse of Luther Clegg, Emeritus Professor of Education

Serves 16

Bake at 350°

2 apples (Granny Smith is best)
2 cans refrigerated crescent rolls
Cinnamon to taste
2 sticks (1 cup) butter
2 cups sugar
splash of vanilla
9 oz. 7-Up or Sprite

Spray 9 x 13-in. pan with Pam. Peel and core apples. Cut each into 8 slices. Unroll crescent rolls and separate each can into 8 pieces. Place one apple slice on each piece at wide end of dough and roll up. Place seam-side down in pan. Sprinkle with cinnamon. In small saucepan melt butter and stir in sugar. Add vanilla and mix well. Pour over rolls. Pour soft drink over this. Bake 30 to 35 minutes. Let sit for 30 minutes to absorb liquid.

Recipe Continues

PER SERVING: Calories 316; Fat 17.5 g (Saturated 9.8 g); Cholesterol 30 mg; Sodium 303 mg; Carbohydrate 41.5 g; Fiber 0.7 g; Sugars 31.3 g; Protein 1.2 g

Banana Cream Pudding

"I got this recipe from Karen Scott in Admissions. I love this recipe because it is great for a party since it feeds several (at least 12) *and you can make it the night before your party, which frees up time the next day."*

Joan Yates, Administrative Assistant, International Admissions

Serves 12

Bake at 375°

Crust:
2 cups graham cracker crumbs (boxed crumbs or 21 square graham crackers, crushed)
⅓ cup melted margarine

Filling:
1 cup (2 sticks) margarine
2 cups confectioner's sugar
2 eggs

Topping:
4 bananas
Cool Whip
chocolate syrup
chopped walnuts

Recipe Continues

Combine graham cracker crumbs and ⅓ cup melted margarine. Spread in 9 x 13-inch pan and bake 5 to 8 minutes. Cool. For filling, beat 2 sticks margarine, confectioner's sugar, and eggs on high speed for 20 minutes. Spread filling over crust. Add 4 bananas, sliced. Spread with Cool Whip and sprinkle with chopped walnuts. Drizzle with chocolate syrup. Refrigerate overnight.

PER SERVING: Calories 385; Fat 26.4 g (Saturated 5.2 g); Cholesterol 27 mg; Sodium 391 mg; Carbohydrate 35.7 g; Fiber 2.4 g; Sugars 20.1 g; Protein 3.4 g

Blackberry Cobbler

"We used to have blackberry bushes in our yard, and Harry would make cobbler from them."

Violet Wickes, Student Accounts, Controller's Office

Serves 8

Bake at 425°

4 cups blackberries
½ tsp. salt
½ cup honey
1 Tbsp. flour
1½ cups biscuit mix
3 Tbsp. sugar
¾ cup milk
2 tsp. sugar to sprinkle on top

In a 1½ quart casserole, toss blackberries with salt, flour, and honey. Mix biscuit mix with sugar and milk. Pour over blackberries. Sprinkle with 2 teaspoons sugar. Bake uncovered 40 minutes or until golden brown.

Recipe Continues

PER SERVING: Calories 218; Fat 4.1 g (Saturated 1.1 g); Cholesterol 2 mg; Sodium 432 mg; Carbohydrate 44 g; Fiber 4.3 g; Sugars 28.6 g; Protein 3.6 g

Book Club Black Forest Cake

"I have made this incredibly easy cake each time I hold the Idyll Tyme Book Club at my home for sixteen women varying in age from sixty-four to eighty-eight years! All club hostesses must have chocolate for club members who expect dessert in advance of rating our monthly book read. Members love the cake's moistness and light taste, and I love making it!"

Carolyn Spence Cagle, Emeritus Professor of Nursing

Serves 16

Bake at 350°

1 box chocolate cake mix (any brand will do)
1 (21-oz.) can cherry or strawberry pie filling
3 eggs
⅓ cup canola oil
vanilla icing or powdered sugar

Mix first four ingredients in mixer for about 3 minutes until well blended. Pour into tube or Bundt pan lightly sprayed with olive or canola oil. Bake for 30 minutes. Cool for 20 minutes on baking rack and use spatula to ease cake out of pan. Cool and drizzle vanilla icing or powdered sugar over cake, as desired.

PER SERVING: Calories 197; Fat 10.8 g (Saturated 1.7 g); Cholesterol 31 mg; Sodium 282 mg; Carbohydrate 25.2 g; Fiber 1 g; Sugars 13.4 g; Protein 3.1 g

Bread Pudding

"My love for bread pudding has had me beg, borrow, and steal (in an accepted manner) from those willing to part with their recipes. My collection includes recipes from a number of countries, including my native Sri Lanka. The basic ingredients in a bread pudding are the same, yet the end result is never quite the same. This bread pudding recipe is a combination of two recipes, which in recent times has taken pride of place in my bread pudding recipe collection, each of which has a story to tell!"

Rosemary Solomons, Director of Classical Music Programming

Serves 4

Bake at 350°

2 Tbsp. unsalted butter for greasing dish
2 cups heavy cream or milk
¼ cup brandy
2 Tbsp. vanilla extract
2 cups of ¼-in. cubes of day-old French bread
2 eggs
¾ cup sugar (light brown or blond palm sugar)
½ cup dark raisins

Topping:
1 cup walnut or pecan pieces, toasted
¼ cup brown sugar
1 Tbsp. ground cinnamon
2 Tbsp. unsalted butter, melted

Bourbon sauce:
½ stick unsalted butter
¼ cup sugar
3 Tbsp. whipping cream
3 Tbsp. bourbon
Pinch of salt

Recipe Continues

Butter the baking dish. Combine cream or milk, brandy, and vanilla in a large bowl. Put bread cubes into bowl and stir to coat. Allow to soak. Using electric mixer on medium, beat eggs and sugar in another bowl until thickened. Egg and sugar mixture should drop in thick ribbons when beaters are lifted. Fold mixture into the bread mixture. Now add the raisins, folding in gently. Transfer pudding into buttered dish. For topping, stir pecan or walnut pieces, brown sugar, cinnamon, and butter in a small bowl until thoroughly combined. Spread evenly over the top of the pudding. Place pudding in baking dish on the middle rack of the oven. Place a larger baking pan filled with a few inches of hot water on the rack beneath. Bake for 55 to 60 minutes or until set. When done, remove from oven and place on a wire rack. Allow to cool completely before serving. Serve with bourbon sauce (if desired).

Bourbon sauce:
Melt butter in a small saucepan over medium heat. Whisk in remaining ingredients. Simmer approximately 3 minutes or until thickened, whisking constantly.

PER SERVING: Calories 1100; Fat 69.8 g (Saturated 32.4 g); Cholesterol 237 mg; Sodium 410 mg; Carbohydrate 96.7 g; Fiber 4.4 g; Sugars 71.7 g; Protein 16 g

Carrot Cake

"This is one of my favorite desserts. My husband makes it for my birthday every year."

Linda Smith, Director, Graduate Program Admissions, Neeley School

Serves 12

Bake at 350°

Recipe Continues

2 cups all-purpose flour
1 cup brown sugar, packed
2 tsp. baking powder
2 tsp. baking soda
1 tsp. salt
½ tsp. nutmeg
2 Tbsp. cinnamon
1 cup sugar
1½ cups canola oil
4 eggs
3 cups shredded carrots
½ cup chopped fresh or canned pineapple, drained
1 cup coconut, optional
1 cup pecans or walnuts, chopped

Cream Cheese Frosting:
1 (8-oz.) package cream cheese
½ cup (1 stick) butter
1 (1-lb.) box 10-X powdered sugar
1 squirt lemon juice

Grease and flour tube pan or sheet cake pan. In a large bowl, combine all dry ingredients. In a small bowl, beat eggs and oil. Add egg mixture to flour mixture. Stir until well blended. Fold in carrot, coconut, pineapple, and nuts. Pour into pan and bake for 25 to 30 minutes, or until a toothpick comes out clean. Serve as is or with cream cheese frosting. Decorate with nuts or raisins.

Frosting:
Mix together all frosting ingredients and spread on cake.

PER SERVING: Calories 699; Fat 38.2 g (Saturated 13 g); Cholesterol 96 mg; Sodium 560 mg; Carbohydrate 86.3 g; Fiber 2.8 g; Sugars 65 g; Protein 6.3 g

Cassata Siciliana

"Every Italian family has a favorite Cassata recipe. This is Joan's family's (the Schifanos) recipe."

Joan Sullivan and Scott Sullivan, Dean of the College of Fine Arts

Serves 8 to 10

1 (16-oz.) or 2 small Sara Lee pound cakes
1 lb. ricotta cheese
2 Tbsp. heavy cream
¼ cup sugar
3 Tbsp. orange-flavored liqueur
3 Tbsp. coarsely chopped candied fruit
2 oz. (½ cup) mini semisweet chocolate chips

Chocolate Frosting
8 oz. semisweet chocolate, cut into pieces, or use chips
½ cup strong black coffee or espresso
⅓ lb. butter, cut into pieces

Cut the cake(s) horizontally into 4 slices. Beat ricotta with electric beater until it is smooth. Beating constantly, add cream, sugar, and liqueur. With rubber spatula, fold in the chopped candied fruit and chocolate chips. Center the bottom slab of the cake on a flat plate and spread generously with the ricotta mixture. Carefully place another slab of cake on top, keeping sides and ends even, and spread with more ricotta. Repeat until all the cake slabs are assembled and the filling has been used up, ending with a plain slice of cake on top. Gently press the loaf together to make it as compact as possible. Do not worry if it feels wobbly; chilling firms the loaf. Refrigerate the Cassata for about 2 hours.

Chocolate frosting:
Melt chocolate with the coffee in a small heavy saucepan or double boiler over low heat, stirring constantly until the chocolate has completely dissolved. Remove pan from the heat and beat in the chilled butter, one

Recipe Continues

piece at a time. Continue beating until the mixture is smooth, then chill the frosting until it thickens to spreading consistency. With a small metal spatula, spread the frosting evenly over the top, sides and ends of the Cassata. Cover loosely with plastic wrap and let the Cassata "ripen" in the refrigerator for at least 24 hours before serving.

PER SERVING: Calories 362; Fat 25.9 g (Saturated 16 g); Cholesterol 91 mg; Sodium 238 mg; Carbohydrate 23.7 g; Fiber 0.3 g; Sugars 15.3 g; Protein 7.9 g

Cheesecake

"I don't recall where I got this recipe unless it was from my mother, who was an excellent cook. When our children grew up enough to enjoy more than chicken nuggets and candy, they loved this cheesecake. They (and my husband) request it for almost every birthday and special occasion. It's different from some other cheesecake recipes in that it is very rich and heavy (but in a good way)."

Nancy Madsen, Director of Donor Relations

Serves 8

Bake at 300°

1 graham cracker crust (baked as directed on box of graham cracker crumbs; you can buy a crust already made, but it's not as good)
12 oz. cream cheese
2 eggs
½ cup sugar
1 tsp. vanilla

Recipe Continues

Topping:
½ pint (1 cup or 8 oz.) sour cream
½ cup sugar
1 tsp. vanilla

Cream eggs, cream cheese, sugar, and vanilla until light and fluffy. Pour in baked crumb shell and bake for 25 minutes. Let cool. Mix sour cream, sugar, and vanilla together. Pour on top of baked mixture. Bake 5 minutes at 300°, or until set. Place cake in refrigerator for at least 2 hours.

PER SERVING: Calories 468; Fat 29.3 g (Saturated 14.9 g); Cholesterol 100 mg; Sodium 327 mg; Carbohydrate 47 g; Fiber 0.5 g; Sugars 36.8 g; Protein 6.7 g

Cherry Cake

"This is an easy Christmas fruit cake which is more like candy. It is a recipe from my Home Economics cooking class at Pershing Junior High School in Houston, and one which our family has enjoyed ever since. These cakes make great gifts, and sealed in Saran Wrap, foil, and a freezer bag will last at least until next Christmas, or until pulled out any time of the year, sliced frozen very thinly, and served with tea or coffee. The slices resemble miniature stained-glass windows."

Judith Oelfke Smith, Associate Director of University Publications
Emmet G. Smith, Emeritus Herndon Professor of Organ and Church Music

Serves about 72

Bake at 300°

1 lb. broken (not chopped) pecans
1 lb. Medjool dates
½ lb. candied red cherries
½ lb. candied green cherries

Recipe Continues

1 lb. golden candied pineapple
1 cup flour
5 eggs
1 cup sugar
2 tsp. vanilla
½ tsp. salt, slightly rounded
A fresh 1½ oz. bottle of lemon extract

Prepare two bread pans or 6 of the smallest foil loaf pans, which make nice gifts, by buttering the pans lightly, then lining them with waxed paper or parchment paper, leaving some paper hanging over the edges. Then butter the lining. In a very large bowl, like a large shallow salad bowl, combine the nuts, dates, and candied fruit, seeding and cutting the dates into several pieces and the cherries into halves. Add the cup of flour and with your hands work it throughout the sticky fruit and nuts, covering them evenly and leaving no flour loose on the bottom of the bowl. In a separate bowl, beat the eggs and sugar together until well combined. Add the vanilla and salt and beat until all is well mixed. Pour the egg mixture over the fruit and, using your hands, mix well so that the egg is distributed evenly throughout the fruit. Then, with your hands, grab handfuls of the mixture and pack into the prepared pans, pressing the fruit together. You can arrange fruit on top to distribute some green and red. If you can find green candied pineapple in flat rings, you can cut them into holly leaves and with the red cherries, decorate the top with a holly sprig. Bake in a preheated oven for an hour or until the tops are slightly toasted. Do not over bake. Cool the cakes on racks for five minutes and then remove them from pans and gently pull off the paper, taking care not to detach fruit on the edges, which can usually be reattached while the cakes are still hot. Turn the cakes right side up and, if using the small foil pans, replace the cakes in their pans. Makes 2 large or 6 small pans.

My addition to the cakes which seems to enhance their flavor is to generously sprinkle drops of lemon extract over the tops of each cake while they are still hot, using the entire 1½-oz. bottle. Then let the cakes cool entirely on racks.

Recipe Continues

Also, I think these cakes are best served frozen, and are certainly easier to slice. Wrap the large cakes in Saran Wrap, then in a large sheet of heavy foil, sealing the edges well, and finally seal them in a freezer bag. For the small fruit cakes, leave them in their pans, cover them well with plastic wrap and foil, and seal them in freezer bags.

PER SERVING: Calories 109; Fat 4.8 g (Saturated 0.5 g); Cholesterol 11 mg; Sodium 22 mg; Carbohydrate 16 g; Fiber 1.6 g; Sugars 12.4 g; Protein 1.5 g

Chocolate Custard Pie

Karen Stone, Director, Brown-Lupton Gallery and spouse of Howard Stone, Professor of Pastoral Theology, Brite School of Divinity

Serves 6 to 8

Bake at 350°

1 pie crust, plus pie weights or dried beans
Scant 2 cups sugar
4 rounded Tbsp. unsweetened dark cocoa powder such as Hershey's Special Dark, sieved
5 Tbsp. unsalted butter, melted
1 oz. 70% dark chocolate, melted with the butter
1 tsp. espresso powder dissolved in 1 Tbsp. hot water (optional)
3 extra large eggs, beaten
¾ cup nonfat evaporated milk, plus generous ¼ cup heavy cream
1½ tsp. vanilla extract or paste
¼ teaspoon salt plus coarse grated sea salt for top
Whipped cream or ice cream to serve

Place crust in large pie plate, crimp edges, and prick all over with a fork. Line with lightweight foil and fill with dry beans or pie weights. Bake

Recipe Continues

15 minutes or until set. Remove weights and foil, bake just a couple of minutes longer until it dries out. While crust is baking, whisk together sugar and cocoa with electric mixer or by hand. Whisk in butter/chocolate mixture, beaten eggs, evaporated milk, cream, vanilla, espresso if using, and ¼ tsp. salt until smooth. Pour filling into pie shell (carefully—it will be very full) and top with coarsely grated sea salt. Cover crust edges with foil and bake on a round pizza pan or rimmed baking sheet for about 45 minutes, until filling is dry around the edges but slightly jiggly. Serve with whipped cream, ice cream, or raspberry sorbet and fresh raspberries.

PER SERVING: Calories 645; Fat 26 g (Saturated 11.3 g); Cholesterol 154 mg; Sodium 474 mg; Carbohydrate 100.3 g; Fiber 2 g; Sugars 86.9 g; Protein 8.8 g

---

Congo Bars

"These were my mother's go-to dessert bars. They routinely showed up at church gatherings, always a big hit."

Cynthia Chapa, German Instructor II

Serves 12

Bake at 350°

2¾ cups sifted flour
½ tsp. salt
2½ tsp. baking powder
⅔ cup shortening or butter
2¼ cups (16-oz. box) brown sugar
3 eggs
1 cup chopped nuts

Recipe Continues

1 (7-oz.) package chocolate chips
1 tsp. vanilla

Mix and sift flour, baking powder, and salt; set aside. Melt shortening together with brown sugar; stir until well mixed. Cool slightly. Add eggs, one at a time, beating well after each addition. Add dry ingredients, then nuts, chocolate chips, and vanilla. Pour into greased pan about 10½ x 15½ x ¾ inches. Bake about 35 minutes. When almost cool, cut into finger-length bars.

PER SERVING: Calories 241; Fat 11.8 g (Saturated 4 g); Cholesterol 22 mg; Sodium 107 mg; Carbohydrate 30.9 g; Fiber 1.2 g; Sugars 17.8 g; Protein 3.8 g

Chocolate Pots de Crème

"My wife Ann received this recipe from a New York friend that she re-met in Fort Worth. It is the easiest and most elegant of desserts."

Pat Miller, Registrar

Serves 4 to 6

1 cup chocolate chips
1½ cup scalded light cream
2 egg yolks
3 Tbsp. brandy

Combine all ingredients in a blender or food processor while cream is still hot. Don't worry about the eggs cooking. The blender or food processor works quickly to handle that problem. Pour into small cups and refrigerate until thickened (several hours to overnight). Top with whipped cream, if desired.

Recipe Continues

PER SERVING: Calories 327; Fat 19.7 g (Saturated 12.7 g); Cholesterol 132 mg; Sodium 67 mg; Carbohydrate 28.1 g; Fiber 1.4 g; Sugars 23.5 g; Protein 5.3 g

Favorite Brownies

"Even as young boys, both of our sons showed an avid interest in cooking. One of them brought this recipe for brownies home from a friend's house after asking his friend's mom to copy it for him. The recipe has served our family well over the years and is now in the recipe files of our three grandchildren. It can be dressed up as dessert by topping a square of it with a scoop of ice cream, a drizzle of chocolate sauce, and a cherry on top."

Mary Jo Clegg, spouse of Luther Clegg, Emeritus Professor of Education

Serves 8 to 12

Bake at 350°

1 cup (2 sticks) butter
4 oz. unsweetened chocolate
¼ cup corn syrup
2 cups sugar
4 eggs, beaten
1½ cups flour
1 tsp. baking powder
1 tsp. vanilla
1 drop or two of peppermint oil (optional)
1 cup walnuts or pecans, coarsely chopped
1½ cups chocolate chips

Melt butter and unsweetened chocolate over low heat and cool. Add corn syrup, sugar, and beaten eggs and mix well. Sift flour, baking pow-

Recipe Continues

der, and salt together in large mixing bowl. Add chocolate mixture and stir until smooth. Stir in vanilla and peppermint oil (if desired) and add nuts and chocolate chips. Spread in 9 x 13-in. pan sprayed with Pam. Bake 30 minutes.

PER SERVING: Calories 873; Fat 51.4 g (Saturated 27 g); Cholesterol 150 mg; Sodium 224 mg; Carbohydrate 100.3. g; Fiber 5.1 g; Sugars 69.4 g; Protein 13.4 g

Glazed Fresh Apple Cookies

"My mother was Thelma Marie Rui Gjelten. Her grandfather, Oskar Rui, emigrated from Norway in the nineteenth century, and her great-great-great-grandfather Karl Rui made Hardanger fiddles. While wearing his ice skates he leaped over teams of horses. This is my mother's recipe. It is a soft cookie, always a big hit."

Karen Stone, Director, Brown-Lupton Gallery and spouse of Howard Stone, Professor of Pastoral Theology, Brite School of Divinity

Makes 24

Bake at 400°

2 cups flour
1 tsp. baking soda
½ cup margarine or butter
1⅓ cups brown sugar
½ tsp. nutmeg
1 tsp. cinnamon
1 tsp. cloves
1 egg
½ cup apple juice

Recipe Continues

1½ cups chopped apples
½ cup raisins or currants
1 cup chopped nuts

Glaze:
1½ cups powdered sugar
1 Tbsp. melted butter
¼ tsp. vanilla
2½ Tbsp. light cream or milk

Mix ingredients, adding apples, raisins, and nuts last. Drop by tablespoons on cookie sheet lined with parchment paper or silicone. Bake for 11 to 14 minutes. Cool slightly, then spread with glaze.
PER SERVING: Calories 176; Fat 8 g (Saturated 1.6 g); Cholesterol 9 mg; Sodium 144 mg; Carbohydrate 24.8 g; Fiber 1.2 g; Sugars 14.3 g; Protein 2.5 g

Grandma's Shortbread

"This is a 'secret' recipe from my mother's family. This is my sister's version, which slightly modifies my grandmother's. It is a bit of work but makes great shortbread (I have some in the freezer right now to nibble on throughout the year)."

Bob Vann, Center for Writing

Makes 24 pieces

Bake at 325°

1 lb. (4 sticks) butter
1 cup plus 1 Tbsp. sugar
1 egg

Recipe Continues

2 lbs. (8 cups) flour—actually use 7½ cups before sifting, then sift flour 3 times to lighten.

Cream butter well. Add sugar and unbeaten egg. Mix well. Very gradually add flour. When all is mixed well, work into a ball. Line 3 round cake pans with wax paper, or use shortbread molds. Divide mixture into 3 equal portions and pat down into each cake pan. (It will take some work to smooth the cakes in the pans.) Prick each all around with a fork and score to cut. Bake for 45 to 50 minutes. Cool in pan. If using shortbread molds, follow baking directions with mold.

PER SERVING (1 PIECE): Calories 310; Fat 15.9 g (Saturated 9.8 g); Cholesterol 47 mg; Sodium 112 mg; Carbohydrate 38 g; Fiber 1 g; Sugars 9.3 g; Protein 4.3 g

Liliko'i "Cheesecake"

"We were served liliko'i cheesecake in Hawaii, and I created this as a close approximation of that delicious and very light dessert. Liliko'i is passion fruit; you can buy passion fruit pulp (Goya is one brand) in the freezer section of many supermarkets."

Karen Stone, Director, Brown-Lupton Gallery and spouse of Howard Stone, Professor of Pastoral Theology, Brite School of Divinity

Serves 8

Crust:
1⅔ cups graham cracker crumbs (or 22 squares finely crushed)
3 Tbsp. honey
¼ cup butter, softened

Recipe Continues

Mix and press firmly into pie plate or 9-inch springform pan.

Filling:
1 envelope unflavored gelatin
½ cup liliko'i (passionfruit) pulp, divided
½ to ¾ cup sugar
½ cup boiling water
1½ (12 oz.) large packages low-fat cream cheese, softened
½ cup sour cream or yogurt

In large bowl, soften gelatin in a little of the juice from the fruit pulp. Mix in sugar. Add boiling water (or juice) and remaining pulp. Stir until gelatin is completely dissolved. Beat in cream cheese until smooth. Stir in sour cream/yogurt. Pour into crust and chill until firm, about 2 hours. (Speed up by placing in freezer for 30 min. before placing in refrigerator.)

PER SERVING: Calories 413; Fat 25.4 g (Saturated 15.1 g); Cholesterol 68 mg; Sodium 286 mg; Carbohydrate 43.2 g; Fiber 1.8 g; Sugars 32.1 g; Protein 6 g

Lazy Mary's Lemon Tart

"A group of us, including the Kleins, Ludvigsons, Bobichs, Watsons, Reineckes, Vanderhoofs, and a local judge and his wife had a dinner club where we met monthly at each other's homes and cooked 'gourmet' food planned by the current hosts. Marianne Bobich was recognized as our outstanding chef."

Joe Bobich, Professor of Chemistry

Serves 8

Bake at 300°

Recipe Continues

1 large, ripe lemon, preferably Meyer
1½ cups confectioner's sugar
¼ lb. unsalted butter
4 large eggs
1 tsp. vanilla
1 8-inch piecrust, preferably graham cracker

Remove any remaining stem end and wash the lemon. Remove seeds and cut into eight pieces (over a food processor bowl to conserve juice). Place lemon pieces into the food processor bowl along with the other ingredients. Puree until smooth (or near it), and pour into piecrust. Bake for 35 to 40 minutes without burning the top. Try to wait until it is cool.

PER SERVING: Calories 352; Fat 20.1 g (Saturated 9.1 g); Cholesterol 118 mg; Sodium 262 mg; Carbohydrate 40.3 g; Fiber 0.6 g; Sugars 32.4 g; Protein 4.3 g

Lemon Buttermilk Chess Pie

"Who doesn't love pie? Some prefer fruit pies with a lattice crust, others crave a cream pie topped with meringue, and those in the south may have a fondness for the fried variety, particularly if it is dusted with powdered sugar. When asked to name my favorite, however, it's no contest. The Lemon Chess Buttermilk Pie baked by my wife Kay is one for the ages. Whether enjoyed around your family table or shared with friends at a potluck dinner, it's sure to please."

Stan Hagadone, Director of Admissions, Brite Divinity School

Serves 8

Bake at 350°

1½ cups sugar

Recipe Continues

1 Tbsp. yellow cornmeal
1 Tbsp. flour
¼ tsp. salt
4 eggs at room temperature
⅓ cup unsalted butter, melted and cooled to room temperature
1 Tbsp. finely grated lemon zest (optional)
⅓ cup lemon juice
½ cup low-fat buttermilk at room temperature
1 tsp. vanilla extract
1 unbaked 9-inch pie crust
1 Tbsp. powdered sugar for garnish

In a small bowl combine the sugar, cornmeal, flour, and salt. In a larger bowl whisk the eggs until lemon colored. Add dry ingredients to the eggs, mixing well. Add melted butter, lemon zest, lemon juice, buttermilk, and vanilla. Beat thoroughly after each addition. Pour into crust and place in oven on middle rack. Bake for 40 minutes until top is golden brown and custard is set. When cool, sprinkle with powdered sugar.

PER SERVING: Calories 273; Fat 11.1 g (Saturated 6.1 g); Cholesterol 103 mg; Sodium 192 mg; Carbohydrate 41.9 g; Fiber 0.1 g; Sugars 39 g; Protein 3.7 g

Lemon Ice Box Pie

"My mother, Esther Winesanker, served this dessert to many guests at small dinner parties, but the event that I remember most was the night that my then fiancé, now husband, first arrived from Los Angeles to meet my family. After tasting this lemon dessert, he announced that he knew he was marrying the right girl, and for years thereafter he enjoyed reminding my mother that he married me for that lemon pie. "

Miriam Levy, daughter of Michael Winesanker, Professor of Musicology and Chair of the Music Department and Esther Winesanker, Library

Recipe Continues

Serves 10 to 12

4 eggs, separated
1 cup sugar, divided
1 large lemon (juice and zest)
1 Tbsp. (1 package) gelatin, dissolved in 3 Tbsp. cold water
3 Tbsp. butter
½ pint whipping cream
2 cups vanilla wafer crumbs (keep some for topping)

Combine in top of double boiler: egg yolks, ½ cup sugar, and juice and zest of lemon. Place over bottom of double boiler in which there is hot water. Cook over low heat, stirring constantly until quite thick. Take top of double boiler away from heat and combine contents with gelatin dissolved in 3 Tbsp. water (dissolve gelatin in water just before you add it, otherwise it stiffens, and make sure you use all of it). Stir in butter and cool. Beat egg whites until quite stiff. Add remaining ½ cup sugar gradually to egg whites. Fold this into cooled lemon mixture. Then fold in stiffly whipped cream. Line greased pie pan (8 inch) with wafer crumbs. Pour in mixture. Top with rest of crumbs. Chill overnight.

PER SERVING: Calories 275; Fat 15.1 g (Saturated 8 g); Cholesterol 109 mg; Sodium 109 mg; Carbohydrate 33.2 g; Fiber 0.5 g; Sugars 26.3 g; Protein 4.2 g

Lemon Sponge Pie

"My grandmother baked this when we came to visit, and it always makes me smile. There was a lot of love in it but my whole family would ask as soon as we came to her house, 'Is there lemon sponge pie?' It was tradition for every holiday."

Linda Moore, Emeritus Professor Social Work

Recipe Continues

Serves 8

Bake at 425°

1 cup sugar
1 Tbsp. melted butter
2 Tbsp. flour
2 egg yolks
Zest and juice of 1 lemon
1 cup milk
2 egg whites, stiffly beaten

Beat together sugar, butter, flour, and egg yolks. Add lemon zest and juice, milk, and egg whites. Mix and bake for at 425° for 15 minutes; reduce heat to 350° and bake another 20 minutes.

PER SERVING: Calories 147; Fat 3.2 g (Saturated 1.7 g); Cholesterol 59 mg; Sodium 35 mg; Carbohydrate 28.2 g; Fiber 0.1 g; Sugars 26.5 g; Protein 2.8 g

Mango and "Whatever" Loaf Cake

"This is a great way to clean out the fridge, or if your friends' gardens are overproducing. It is very moist and delicious, similar to a quick bread but too wonderful for that; I'm calling it a cake, like the French do."

Karen Stone, Director, Brown-Lupton Gallery and spouse of Howard Stone, Professor of Pastoral Theology, Brite School of Divinity

Serves about 32

Bake at 350°

Recipe Continues

4 cups flour, stirred
½ tsp. salt
1 Tbsp. plus 1 tsp. baking soda
1 Tbsp. cinnamon
3 cups sugar
½ cup vegetable oil (olive oil is too strong, but avocado oil or liquid coconut oil is delicious)
7 eggs, beaten
Mashed overripe mangoes, for the largest part, plus grated zucchini or other squash, mashed overripe bananas, grated apple, or whatever else you think will work, to make 4 to 5 cup mixture
¾ cup chopped dates, raisins, or dried cranberries
1 cup coarsely chopped pecans or walnuts
1 cup flaked coconut

Grease four medium-sized bread pans with butter and coat with flour, or use silicone pans. Whisk flour, salt, and soda together in a huge bowl. Stir in the rest of the ingredients and ladle into pans. Bake for 45 minutes or until knife or skewer inserted in center comes out clean. Leave in pans for about 10 minutes, then remove from pans and cool on their sides on wire cooling racks. Fabulous with or without butter! If you want this to be more of a dessert, drizzle slices with icing or serve with ice cream.

PER SERVING: Calories 281; Fat 8.2 g (Saturated 2.4 g); Cholesterol 48 mg; Sodium 71 mg; Carbohydrate 50.2 g; Fiber 2 g; Sugars 32.7 g; Protein 4.4 g

Margaret's Praline Cookies

"Dr. Margaret Rouse was chair of the School of Ed's Elementary Department when my husband joined the faculty at TCU in 1968. She quickly became his mentor and our family friend. Margaret was not known for her culinary prowess and often told funny anecdotes of her failures—such as attempting to make a pie but discovering, just as company was scheduled to arrive, that the filling had escaped the oven, dripped onto the floor, and was willfully heading for the back door. However, Margaret had an ace up her sleeve in her praline cookies. The recipe was a family favorite. Margaret used it for years because it was easy, delicious, and practically foolproof. She passed it to me, and the cookies became one of my husband's favorites."

Mary Jo Clegg, spouse of Luther Clegg, Emeritus Professor of Education

Serves 24

Bake at 350°

12 double graham crackers
1 cup (2 sticks) butter
1 cup light brown sugar, firmly packed
1 cup pecans, chopped

Line bottom of a rimmed cookie sheet with 12 double graham crackers. Combine butter and brown sugar in pan and bring to a boil over medium heat. Cook for one minute. Remove from heat. Add pecans. Stir well. Pour syrup over graham crackers. Bake for 10 minutes. When cool, cut into squares.

PER SERVING: Calories 129; Fat 9.3 g (Saturated 5.1 g); Cholesterol 20 mg; Sodium 99 mg; Carbohydrate 11.5 g; Fiber 0.3 g; Sugars 8.1 g; Protein 0.7 g

Miss Blanche's Pecan Pie

"The recipe originally belonged to Miss Blanche, a lady who came to Longhorn Valley as a mail-order bride. She rode the train from Georgia to Colorado City, Texas, more than a hundred years ago to marry Mr. Adair, a former buffalo hunter living in the Valley. Miss Blanche brought with her a friend, Miss Lila Foote, because Mr. Adair had written Miss Blanche of his friend, Mr. Louis Poteet, also a bachelor in need of a wife. Miss Blanche and Miss Foote found the two men 'acceptable,' and the two couples were married. Mr. Poteet became my husband's grandfather."

Mary Jo Clegg, spouse of Luther Clegg, Emeritus Professor of Education

Serves 8

Bake at 350°

1 unbaked pie shell
1 cup sugar
1 cup dark Karo syrup
¼ tsp. salt
3 eggs, lightly beaten
⅓ cup butter, melted
1 tsp. vanilla
1 heaping cup of pecans (whole or coarsely broken)

Mix sugar and salt. Stir in beaten eggs. Add melted butter and vanilla and stir until smooth. Fold in pecans. Pour into unbaked pie shell and bake for 50 to 60 minutes, or until a knife inserted in the center comes out clean.

PER SERVING: Calories 414; Fat 17.2 g (Saturated 7.3 g); Cholesterol 82 mg; Sodium 298 mg; Carbohydrate 64.5 g; Fiber 0.5 g; Sugars 37 g; Protein 3.2 g

Mom's Saucepan Brownies

"When my husband, Augie, was about twelve years old, he was often bugging his mother to make brownies. One day she said to him, 'If you want them so badly, learn to make them.' So he did, with a little help from his mom, like learning to stir in the flour slowly so as not to have it fly everywhere. It was the first recipe he learned to cook. It came out of a 1951 Woman's Day *magazine kept in the recipe drawer. Friends and family devour them regardless of calories."*

Suzanne Huffman, Emeritus Professor, Schieffer College of Communication

Serves 12

Bake at 325°

⅓ cup shortening
2 squares (2 oz.) unsweetened chocolate
½ tsp. vanilla
1 cup sugar
2 eggs
¾ cup sifted flour
¼ tsp. salt
¾ cup chopped nuts

Melt shortening and chocolate in saucepan over low heat. Cool. Beat in vanilla and sugar. Add eggs, one at a time, beating well after each. In a separate bowl sift flour and salt together; add nuts. Blend chocolate mixture into dry ingredients, mixing well. Bake in greased and floured 8 x 8 x 2-in. pan for 25 minutes. Cool a few minutes and cut in squares.

PER SERVING: Calories 227; Fat 13.4 g (Saturated 4.1 g); Cholesterol 27 mg; Sodium 119 mg; Carbohydrate 26.3 g; Fiber 1.8 g; Sugars 17.2 g; Protein 3.8 g

Peach Cobbler (fresh)

"Having grown up in Northern California surrounded by orchards, many of my favorite recipes involve fruit. Two family favorites that came with me when we moved from California to Texas in 1976 are made with peaches. This is especially fitting since, upon my retirement in 2004, we moved from Fort Worth to Weatherford, which was named the Peach Capital of Texas by the state legislature in 1991. Those of us in the library and others across campus looked forward every summer to Dr. Paul (Dept. of Religion) and Ruth (library) Wassenich coming to the library parking lot to deliver boxes and bags of peaches from their orchard. The cobbler topping recipe was from my mother-in-law and the peach crisp recipe was from my secret sister in a social/service sorority that I once belonged to."

Janet Douglass, Periodicals Librarian, Mary Couts Burnett Library

Serves 8

Bake at 400°

4 cups peeled, sliced fresh peaches
1 Tbsp. cornstarch
½ cup sugar
¼ tsp. cinnamon

or

1 (1 lb. 13 oz.) can sliced peaches with syrup
3 Tbsp. cornstarch
½ tsp. cinnamon

Cobbler topping:
1 cup flour
⅔ cup sugar
1 tsp. baking powder
½ tsp. salt
½ tsp. cinnamon

Recipe Continues

1 egg, beaten
½ cup oil
½ tsp. vanilla

Mix sugar (if using fresh peaches), peaches, cornstarch, and cinnamon in medium saucepan. Cook, stirring constantly, until mixture thickens and boils for one minute. Pour into 2-quart casserole. Mix together topping ingredients. Drop six spoonsful of topping onto hot fruit. Bake for 25 to 30 minutes. Serve warm.

Alternative: Fresh Peach Crisp

Bake at 375°

Peel and slice 6 to 8 peaches into 10-inch Pyrex pie dish or 8 x 8 x 2-in. baking dish.

Topping:
1 cup flour
1 cup sugar
¼ tsp. salt.
½ tsp. cinnamon
½ cup butter, softened
Mix topping ingredients together, put on top of peaches, and bake 45 to 50 minutes

Note: To make fresh peaches easy to peel, use a slotted spoon to dip each peach into boiling water for 5 or 6 seconds, then plunge into a large bowl of ice water (use lots of ice and replenish as it melts). Transfer each batch of peaches into another bowl after they have been in the ice water several minutes. The skins will easily strip off, wasting none of the fruit.

PER SERVING: Calories 296; Fat 14.4 g (Saturated 2 g); Cholesterol 20 mg; Sodium 156 mg; Carbohydrate 39.3 g; Fiber 0.9 g; Sugars 23.8 g; Protein 2.8 g

Peanut Brittle

"My mother-in-law was a great cook, and she seldom used a recipe. One time when she was making this, her ten-year-old grandson pulled up a chair beside her and copied the ingredients as she added them. Thus, he created a recipe."

Gail Davis, Emeritus Professor of Nursing

Serves 8

2 cups sugar
1 cup water
1 cup white corn syrup
2 cups raw peanuts
1 tsp. vanilla
1 Tbsp. butter
½ tsp. baking soda

Cook the sugar, water, and syrup to the "soft ball" stage (235° to 240°) on a candy thermometer. Add peanuts and cook to the "hard crack" (300° to 310°) stage on a candy thermometer. Remove from heat. Add vanilla, butter, and baking soda. Stir well and quickly. Pour on a buttered cookie sheet. Cool and break into pieces.

PER SERVING: Calories 518; Fat 19.4 g (Saturated 3.4 g); Cholesterol 2 mg; Sodium 98 mg; Carbohydrate 85.4 g; Fiber 3.1 g; Sugars 61.7 g; Protein 9.4 g

Pepper Nuts

"Since this recipe makes so many cookies, I share them as Christmas gifts with friends and coworkers. My son, Rob Allen, now makes these and takes them to share with his colleagues in the TCU IT office."

Phyllis Allen, Professor of Nursing and Coordinator of Basic Skills Learning Lab

Serves 10 to 15

Bake at 400°

3 cups flour
1½ cups sugar
2 tsp. cinnamon
1 tsp. ginger
½ tsp. cloves
1 cup (2 sticks) butter
2 Tbsp. dark Karo syrup
1 egg
2 tsp. baking soda
1 Tbsp. warm water

Sift flour, sugar, cinnamon, ginger, and cloves. Add butter, syrup, and egg; mix well. Dissolve baking soda in water and combine with mixture. On floured surface, roll pieces of dough into 12-inch-long ropes about the size of a finger. Chill overnight. Slice into ¼-inch pieces and place on ungreased cookie sheet. Bake for 5 to 7 minutes. Depending on the size of the rolls of dough, this makes a lot of small cookies.

PER SERVING: Calories 228; Fat 0.8 g (Saturated 0.2 g); Cholesterol 16 mg; Sodium 7 mg; Carbohydrate 51.5 g; Fiber 1 g; Sugars 21.1 g; Protein 4.4 g

Pineapple Pie

"This is a family recipe passed down from my mother-in-law, Viva May. Always a family hit for all occasions, with everyone calling dibs on the last piece."

Joe Ann May, Financial Assistant, Financial Services Department

Serves 8

Bake at 350°

1½ cups sugar
½ cup (1 stick) butter
1 (8-oz.) can crushed pineapple
3 Tbsp. flour
1 tsp. vanilla
2 eggs
1 unbaked 9-inch pie shell

If desired, cover edges of unbaked pie shell with aluminum foil to prevent over-browning. Beat all ingredients together; pour into pie shell and bake for 50 minutes, or until set and brown on top.

PER SERVING: Calories 362; Fat 17.9 g (Saturated 8.4 g); Cholesterol 71 mg; Sodium 200 mg; Carbohydrate 50.4 g; Fiber 0.5 g; Sugars 40.4 g; Protein 2.6 g

Pumpkin Chiffon Pie

"When my mother-in-law, Minnie Lee Sharbar Dromgoole, heard my strong opposition to pumpkin pie, she searched through her massive collection of recipes and found one called Pumpkin Chiffon Pie, which she claimed I would like. I doubted it, but after one bite I knew she was right. Who knew chiffon could make pumpkin taste so yummy? I made

Recipe Continues

Pumpkin Chiffon Pie, mostly for holidays, for many years after that. Now, my daughter, Jenn LeBow, has taken over the role of making her grandmother's recipe for family holidays."

Maggie Thomas, Emeritus Professor of Journalism

Serves 8

1 Tbsp. unflavored gelatin (1 package)
¼ cup cold water
½ cup milk
1 cup sugar
1¼ cups pumpkin
3 egg yolks, lightly beaten
3 egg whites
½ tsp. each: salt, cinnamon, and ginger
½ cup whipping cream
Cooked 9-inch pie crust (deep dish is best)

Dissolve gelatin in water. In the top of a double boiler, combine milk, ½ cup sugar, pumpkin, egg yolks, and spices. Cook over boiling water until thick. Remove from heat, add gelatin, and stir until gelatin is completely dissolved. Place in refrigerator. Meanwhile beat egg whites with remaining ½ cup sugar, adding 1 Tbsp. of sugar at a time, as for meringue. Whip cream. When pumpkin mixture begins to set, stir in egg white mixture and whipped cream until no white is visible. Pour into pie crust and refrigerate until fully set.

PER SERVING: Calories 173; Fat 4.9 g (Saturated 2.4 g); Cholesterol 71 mg; Sodium 193 mg; Carbohydrate 30.3 g; Fiber 1.1 g; Sugars 27.2 g; Protein 4 g

Rocky Road Goodies

"Loretta Pierce was an administrative assistant in the School of Education at TCU. Attractive, smart, friendly, and charming, she was a favorite among faculty and staff. She brought these 'goodies' to the faculty workroom to share one Christmas, and they were so popular, she passed around the recipe. Loretta unfortunately died of cancer much too early, but her memory is lovingly alive."

Mary Jo Clegg, spouse of Luther Clegg, Emeritus Professor of Education

Serves 12 to 16

1 (12-oz.) package chocolate chips
1 (14-oz.) can Eagle Brand sweetened condensed milk
2 Tbsp. butter
1 (10-oz.) package miniature marshmallows
1½ cups nuts

Melt chocolate and milk in double boiler. Take off heat and add remaining ingredients. Mix and pour into greased 9 x 13-in. buttered pan or dish. Refrigerate until set and cut into squares.

PER SERVING: Calories 446; Fat 20.5 g (Saturated 9.1 g); Cholesterol 16 mg; Sodium 203 mg; Carbohydrate 59.8 g; Fiber 2.5 g; Sugars 46.4 g; Protein 7.9 g

Salted Tropical Toffee Crisps

"This is Howard's favorite cookie, also the fave of many other people we know! I got the idea and some of the chemistry from America's Test Kitchen, but made many changes along the way to bump up the flavor."

Karen Stone, Director, Brown-Lupton Gallery and spouse of Howard Stone, Professor of Pastoral Theology, Brite School of Divinity

Makes 90 to 100

Bake at 350°

2 cups all-purpose flour
1½ tsp. baking powder—sift if lumpy
1 tsp. baking soda—sift if lumpy
3½ sticks softened, unsalted butter
2 cups dark brown sugar
½ cup white sugar
2 large eggs
2 tsp. vanilla
4 cups old-fashioned rolled oats
2 cups flaked coconut
1½ cups coarsely chopped macadamia nuts
Grated zest of 3 limes or more—don't be shy (see notes)
Coarse sea salt

Line 3 or 4 cookie sheets with parchment paper. Whisk together flour, baking powder, and baking soda. Beat butter and sugar in mixer with paddle attachment until thoroughly mixed and light, approximately 2 minutes. Add egg and vanilla and beat on medium about 30 seconds. Scrape down bowl. With mixer running at low, add flour mixture little by little, then keep mixer running and add oats, nuts, coconut, and lime zest until well mixed. Using a scant level cookie scoop, set dough on cookie sheet. (It is possible to get 18 cookies to a sheet in alternating 4/3 rows if you don't mind a few occasionally running together.) Press down with hands that have been sprayed with nonstick spray. Sprinkle

Recipe Continues

each cookie with a few flakes of coarse sea salt. Bake one sheet at a time until golden brown and crispy, about 15 to 18 minutes, depending on your oven. Do not under-bake. Leave cookies on the pan until they are completely cool. You can re-use the parchment paper one time.

There are endless possible variations, for example:
Lemon-almond: Instead of lime zest and macadamia nuts, use zest of 2 large lemons and sliced or slivered almonds.
Pecan-tangerine: Substitute zest of 2 tangerines or 4 mandarin oranges and broken pecans.
Walnut-orange: Substitute zest of 2 oranges and coarsely broken walnuts.
Use your imagination! It is always okay to use more citrus zest than the recipe calls for.

PER SERVING: Calories 249; Fat 19.3 g (Saturated 6.9 g); Cholesterol 24 mg; Sodium 117 mg; Carbohydrate 18.7 g; Fiber 2.4 g; Sugars 8.6 g; Protein 3 g

Screwball Cake

"This is the best chocolate cake ever and great fun to bake with kids. My sisters and I always fought over who got to fill the holes and who got to pour the water. Now my granddaughter and I can do it together and she gets all the fun. It's also a cake without eggs—that is screwball. My cousin and I still talk about it after more than sixty years."

Linda Moore, Emeritus Professor of Social Work

Serves 8 to 10

Bake at 350°

3 cups flour
2 cups sugar
⅔ cups cocoa

Recipe Continues

2 tsp. baking soda
1 tsp. salt
2 tsp. vinegar
2 tsp. vanilla
1 cup vegetable oil
2 cups cold water

Mix together flour, sugar, cocoa, baking soda, and salt. Make 3 holes in the dry mixture. Place vinegar in the first hole, vanilla in the second hole, and oil in the third hole. Pour water over all and mix. We always use 3 round pans, but if you make a large rectangle I would divide it into 3 sections and stack them. People can do what they want but kids love the 3 layers! Grease and flour the pans. Bake until a toothpick comes out clean (30 to 35 min).

Almost any icing works. I'm a fan of buttercream but you can do any flavor and add sprinkles or chocolate chips or whatever works for the kids. This cake is best refrigerated. It is super moist and never dries out. Makes a 3-layer cake.

PER SERVING: Calories 618; Fat 28.7 g (Saturated 6 g); Cholesterol 0 mg; Sodium 608 mg; Carbohydrate 89.8 g; Fiber 3.4 g; Sugars 50 g; Protein 6.1 g

Sopapilla Cheesecake

"A friend gave me this recipe when she fixed it for a Cinco de Mayo party. It has now become a favorite birthday cake for one of my granddaughters."

Phyllis Allen, Coordinator of the Skills Lab for Harris College of Nursing and Health Sciences

Serves 12

Recipe Continues

Bake at 350°

2 (8-oz.) cans of crescent rolls
2 (8-oz.) packages of cream cheese
½ cup (1 stick) butter
1½ cups sugar
1 tsp. vanilla
1 tsp. cinnamon

Using a 9 x 13-in. pan, spread 1 can of crescent rolls on the bottom. Mix cream cheese, 1 cup sugar, and vanilla. Spread cream cheese mixture on rolls. Cover with second can of crescent rolls. Heat butter, ½ cup sugar and cinnamon together. Pour over the top roll layer. Bake for 30 minutes.

PER SERVING: Calories 311; Fat 21.8 g (Saturated 13.6 g); Cholesterol 62 mg; Sodium 203 mg; Carbohydrate 28 g; Fiber 0.1 g; Sugars 25.6 g; Protein 3.1 g

Swedish Pastry

"This is a recipe from the Swedish Hospital in Minneapolis, MN. It was acquired while I was working there is the 1960s. It was served in the coffee shop every Wednesday, and it was so good it drew my husband and friends. The Swedish Hospital is no longer there; it has been replaced by the newer Metropolitan Medical Center."

Gail Davis, Emeritus Professor of Nursing

Serves 6

Bake at 375°

Pie crust:
1 cup flour

Recipe Continues

½ cup (1 stick) butter
2 Tbsp. cold water

Filling:
1 cup boiling water
1 cup flour
½ cup (1 stick) butter
3 eggs
1 tsp. almond extract

Make a piecrust from flour, butter, and water and spread in the bottom of a 9 x 9-in. pan.

For filling: Add butter to boiling water and stir until butter is melted. Remove from burner and add flour. Stir until smooth. Add eggs, one at a time, stirring until smooth after each addition. Add almond extract. Spread mixture over crust and bake 45 minutes. Spread with powdered sugar icing (mix a small amount of milk with powdered sugar).

PER SERVING: Calories 456; Fat 33.3 g (Saturated 25.2 g); Cholesterol 163 mg; Sodium 250 mg; Carbohydrate 32.1 g; Fiber 1.1 g; Sugars 0.4 g; Protein 7.4 g

Vanilla Chip Fruit Tart

"This dessert looks as good as it tastes. You can easily arrange the fruit to match any celebration."

Donna Johnson, Provost's Office

Serves 10 to 12

Bake at 300°

Recipe Continues

Crust:
¾ cup butter or margarine, softened
½ cup confectioner's sugar
1½ cups all-purpose flour

Vanilla filling:
1 (10-oz.) package white chocolate chips
¼ cup whipping cream
1 (8-oz.) package cream cheese, softened

Fruit topping:
¼ cup sugar
1 Tbsp. cornstarch
½ cup pineapple juice
½ tsp. lemon juice
Assorted fresh fruit (soft): kiwi, mandarin oranges, strawberries, blueberries, raspberries, peaches, etc.

Beat butter and sugar until light and fluffy; blend in flour. Press mixture onto bottom and up side of 12-inch round pizza pan. Bake 20 to 25 minutes or until lightly browned. Cool completely.

Filling: In microwave-safe bowl, microwave vanilla chips and whipping cream at high 1 to 1½ minutes or until chips are melted and mixture is smooth when stirred. Beat in cream cheese. Spread over cooled crust.

Topping: In small saucepan combine sugar and cornstarch; stir in juices. Cook over medium heat, stirring constantly until thickened; cool. Meanwhile, slice and arrange fruit on top of filling; pour juice mixture over fruit and chill before serving.

PER SERVING: Calories 447; Fat 31.9 g (Saturated 19.8 g); Cholesterol 71 mg; Sodium 193 mg; Carbohydrate 36.8 g; Fiber 0.6 g; Sugars 25.1 g; Protein 5 g

Appendix: Recipe Substitutions for Healthy Deliciousness

To reduce fat and calories:

Instead of using:	Substitute with:
Butter in baking	Unsweetened applesauce, pureed banana, or baby food
Oil or butter for sautéing	Cooking spray
Cream cheese	Pureed low-fat cottage cheese
Whole egg in baking	Two egg whites
Potato chips	Kale chips

To replace fat with a healthier option:

Instead of using:	Substitute with:
Mayonnaise in a dip or sauce	Avocado puree or Greek yogurt
Mayonnaise in a salad dressing	Pureed canned white beans
Mayonnaise on a sandwich	Mustard
Sour cream	Low-fat yogurt
Oil or butter for sautéing	Chicken or vegetable broth

To reduce sodium:

Instead of using:	Substitute with:
Garlic salt or onion salt	Garlic powder or onion powder
Seasoning salt	Herb-blend seasonings
Salt	Lemon (or any citrus) juice or hot sauce
Tomato sauce on pizza	Sliced fresh tomatoes
Soy sauce	Low-sodium soy sauce

To make a gluten-free option of a recipe:

Instead of using:	Substitute with:
Bread crumbs for a topping	Rolled oats, rice cereal, or crushed corn chips
Flour in a white sauce	Cornstarch
Flour in baked goods	Almond flour or canned black beans
Wheat macaroni	Pasta made with quinoa, corn, rice, or beans
Spaghetti or noodles	Spiralized vegetables ("zoodles") or spaghetti squash
Flour tortilla	Corn tortilla
Couscous	Quinoa
Bread for a sandwich	Lettuce wraps
Croutons to top a salad	Roasted nuts
Soy sauce	Tamari sauce

To reduce sugar:

Instead of using:	Substitute with:
Soft drinks or soda	Seltzer water
Chocolate chips	Cacao nibs
Sugar in a recipe	Cut half and replace with 1 tsp. vanilla extract
Sugar in coffee	Ground cinnamon
Syrup for pancakes	Pureed fruit

Index